PowerPoint 97

Sue Coles

Department of Business and Management Studies
Crewe and Alsager Faculty
Manchester Metropolitan University

Jenny Rowley

School of Management and Social Sciences
Edge Hill University College

Letts

1998

Acknowledgments

We have appreciated the opportunity to continue to experiment with and write about the products in the Microsoft suite of applications software and hope that this book will encourage others to enjoy this software and to use 'more than ten per cent' of its functionality. Of course, while we have been 'playing with computers' our family and colleagues have at times needed to be patient. We would like to acknowledge the contributions of Martyn, Peter, Helen, Shula, Lynsey and Zeta.

PowerPoint, Windows 95™, Excel™ and Access™ © Microsoft Corporation, all rights reserved. Screen displays from PowerPoint, Access 7, Excel 97 and Windows 95 reprinted with permission from Microsoft Corporation.

A CIP record for this book is available from the British Library.

ISBN 1 85805 358 7

Editorial and production services: Genesys Editorial Limited

Typeset by Kai, Nottingham

Printed in Great Britain by Ashford Colour Press, Gosport

Contents

About this book

Aims

PowerPoint is a sophisticated presentations package which is part of the Microsoft Office suite of applications software. This book is intended for any new user of PowerPoint who needs to acquire a good working knowledge of PowerPoint in order to create presentations and accompanying materials, such as handouts and notes. Such users will include students, managers and other professionals in both business and community contexts. The book covers the creation of slides, on screen presentations and autorunning presentations. It is equally suitable for use by students in the classroom or open learning workshop, or by the general user for home study. The book assumes some familiarity with the basics of word processing, preferably in the context of Word 97. The Letts publication *Word 97 Basic Skills* will be useful if you are not already familiar with Word 97. The book can be used:

- as part of a course
- for independent study
- for reference.

Structure

This book introduces you to the basics of the creation of presentations through a series of applications oriented tasks. A series of self contained units takes you through the production of various presentations of different types and gradually introduces the features and functions of the presentations package. Each session includes a number of tasks. These create and gradually refine a small number of presentations. These presentations are variously based on themes associated with two hypothetical organisations, Chelmer Leisure and Chelmer Estates. One presentation takes the form of the slides to accompany a monthly staff briefing, and another the slides to accompany a consultant's presentation on a proposal for a new project. Two of the other presentations are autorunning presentations that might be used on screen in an entrance foyer or public office area. As you work through the book you will build these presentations by adding additional slides of features. Each unit takes approximately one hour to complete.

This book has 20 units. These are structured in such a way that you can very quickly learn how to create a presentation using many of the 'default' or 'standard' settings available within PowerPoint. Later units encourage you to explore the wide ranging multi media capabilities of PowerPoint more fully.

To do this	Turn to
Understand the features of PowerPoint	Unit 1 Overview of PowerPoint
Create a new presentation	Unit 2 Creating a new presentation
Learn how to use the different views	Unit 3 Understanding PowerPoint views

Create a presentation from a blank presentation and apply templates	Unit 4 Using Blank Presentations and templates
Control the look and layout of a presentation	Unit 5 Applying Looks and Layouts; using Masters
Create notes and handouts	Unit 6 Working with Notes and Handouts
Improve the formatting of your text	Unit 7 Formatting text
Use tables and borders on slides	Unit 8 Using tables and borders
Use text boxes	Unit 9 Using text boxes
Add clip art and WordAart	Unit 10 Using clip art and WordArt
Apply colour schemes and backgrounds	Unit 11 Colour schemes and backgrounds
Creating and inserting a chart	Unit 12 Adding charts
Using the drawing tools	Unit 13 Using the drawing tools
Importing and exporting objects	Unit 14 Importing and exporting
Create an autorunning presentation	Unit 15 Autorunning presentations
Apply animation and create slides	Unit 16 Animations
Add an organisational chart	Unit 17 Organisational Charts
Design specialist slides and effects	Unit 18 Specialist slides and effects
Create custom slide designs	Unit 19 Creating custom slide designs
Present slide shows using computers that do not have PowerPoint installed	Unit 20 PowerPoint Viewer; Internet links

Two appendices, Quick Reference 1 and Quick Reference 2, summarise, respectively, basic Windows operations and PowerPoint toolbars.

What else do you need?

To carry out the activities in this book you will need a PC running Windows 95 and Office 97.

A note to lecturers and students

This book introduces the basics of presentation design through a series of application oriented tasks. The approach does not assume any previous knowledge of the creation of presentations, and indeed PowerPoint offers some ideas concerning the structuring of different types of presentations for the benefit of relative novices to presentation creation.

Readers who are familiar with the Windows 95 environment, and in particular with Word, will find it much easier to familiarise themselves with PowerPoint, since many of the features that are used in PowerPoint, such as table and borders, and charts and drawing objects are also available in Word. Conversely, experience in handling such objects and features in PowerPoint will extend the students' ability to create sophisticated and professionally designed word processed documents.

This book may be used as a basis for independent study or for class activities. In either instance it is important to:

- work methodologically through the tasks in the order in which they are presented; text and objects created in earlier tasks may be used in later ones

- take time for rest and reflection and break learning into manageable sessions

- think about what you are doing

- expect to make mistakes; think about the consequences of any mistakes and learn from them.

Lecturers' disk

A $3\frac{1}{2}''$ disk is available (free of charge to lecturers recommending the book as a course text) containing extracts from some of the presentations that are created through the tasks in this book.

Conventions

The following conventions have been adopted to distinguish between the various objects on the screen.

- Dialog box names, menu items and commands are shown as File-Exit, which means choose the File menu and then select the option Exit from that menu.

- Buttons, tabs and icons are shown in bold inside shaded rectangles, e.g. **Cancel**

- Keys are shown in underlined italics e.g. *Ctrl*

- Filenames are shown in bold e.g. **Termref**

- Text you type yourself is shown in bold italic, e.g. enter **Chelmer Estates**.

 Indicates a tip providing a helpful hint

 Indicates a cautionary note

 Indicates a cross reference.

Overview of PowerPoint

What you will learn in this unit

This unit introduces PowerPoint and looks at good practice in the creation of presentations. It starts by explaining how PowerPoint can assist in the preparation of presentations and then reviews some practical considerations concerning the creation of presentations. The unit concludes with a brief overview of the PowerPoint main window and the facilities for accessing the Office Assistant and tutorial system. By the end of this unit you will be able to:

- understand the potential uses and facilities of PowerPoint
- identify some contexts in which presentations might be created
- be aware of some of the practical considerations associated with presentations
- understand the PowerPoint main window
- be able to access help in PowerPoint.

What is PowerPoint?

PowerPoint is a presentation graphics software package, that is, it is a software package designed to help you to create presentations for your audience. These presentations graphics may support your own in-person presentation or they form an independent autorunning presentation. There are a wide variety of different contexts in which it is necessary to create presentations. For students, these include:

- giving a group presentation about a project
- giving a seminar paper
- making a short presentation as part of a viva or oral examination
- giving a demonstration of, say, a computer project
- creating an autorunning presentation for use in a poster session or simulated trade fair.

In the business world, presentations may form part of:

- a job interview
- a sales meeting
- a consultancy briefing
- a team briefing
- a public lecture
- an exhibition stand display.

A presentation software package makes your presentations more professional. If you are not accustomed to giving presentations and feel a little uncomfortable in the situation, a good set of slides or, most professionally, an autorunning slide show can lend confidence and help you to impress your audience.

Task 1: Preparing for a presentation

Make a list of the contexts in which you are likely to create presentations over the next few months. Select one of these contexts and identify:

■ the length of the presentation

■ the audience

■ the type of presentation graphics that you might need.

PowerPoint facilities

PowerPoint offers facilities for text handling, outlining, drawing, graphing, clip art, and sound. In addition, it is easy to import text and data created in the other Office applications into a PowerPoint presentation.

PowerPoint can be used to create:

■ overhead transparency slides (colour or black and white)

■ 35mm slides

■ on-screen presentations

■ autorunning on-screen presentations

■ videoconferencing

■ on-disk presentation for sending to a colleague for remote viewing.

In addition to the content of the presentation that is displayed to the audience, PowerPoint also supports the creation of handouts, speaker's notes and outlines. More specifically, it offers the following features.

■ *Presentation* – a collection of slides, speaker's handouts, speaker's notes and outline, all in one file.

■ *Slides* – the individual 'pages' of your presentation. Slides may be overhead transparencies or 35mm slides.

■ *Handouts* – support your presentation. They are smaller, printed versions of your slides, either two, three or six to a page. As required, additional information such as company name, date and page numbers can be printed on each page.

■ *Speaker's notes* – your personal notes to assist you in delivering the presentation. They can be entered in association with a specific slide and are printed on a page underneath a copy of the appropriate slide.

■ *Outlines* – provide a summary of the presentation, and can be useful while you are developing your presentation. In the outline, your titles and main text appear, but not the art or the text typed with the Text tool.

Assistance in creating new presentations

PowerPoint offers a number of facilities that help you to create a set of slides that have a professional and consistent appearance. You will encounter the following terms on many occasions later in this set of units.

Design – a design (previously termed template in earlier versions of Powerpoint) is a presentation in which the masters and the colours have been especially designed for a particular 'look'. Designs define what your text will look like and where it will appear, and they offer a complete colour scheme. PowerPoint comes with many ready made designs. It is also possible to create new designs by creating a presentation with a specific look, and then using that presentation design as a template for a subsequent presentation.

Title and Slide Masters – hold the format for the title and following slides. Text, together with any background items that should appear on your slides, such as a logo can be included on these masters. Any change to the slide master will affect all of the slides in your presentation that follow the slide master formatting.

Handout Master – performs a similar function for handouts to that which the Slide Master performs for slides.

Notes Master – performs a similar function for notes to that which the Slide Master performs for slides.

The Office Assistant

Click on the **Office Assistant** button to display the Office Assistant. The Office Assistant is an animated graphic that appears in a window of its own, it also alerts you by using sound. When you have a question about how to do something you can ask the Office Assistant, for example, 'How do I add clipart to a slide?'. To do this click on the Assistant window and key your question into the What would you like to do box and click on the **Search** button.

The Assistant can, if you wish, provide Help with tasks as you perform them without the need to ask questions.

Steps in creating effective presentations with PowerPoint

This activity provides a step by step guide to organising your approach to using PowerPoint. We then visit some important features for creating presentations.

Using PowerPoint to create presentations

On the first few occasions that you use PowerPoint the range of facilities can appear daunting. These few simple steps outline how you should go about creating a presentation. Essentially the sequence is to organise your ideas first, then enter them into PowerPoint, and later format the slides and draw them together as a presentation.

Plan, organise and enter your ideas There are a number of different ways of doing this.

- Write the ideas down on paper and later enter them either into a blank document or use the assistance of the AutoContent Wizard.

- Enter the text of your presentation into a Word document and then import the text into PowerPoint.

- Open a blank presentation in PowerPoint and simply enter the text or incorporate slides from other presentations.

- Use the AutoContent Wizard to help you structure your ideas, if this Wizard is applicable.

Edit and arrange your contents Refine your content by editing and rearranging text in Outline and Slide Views.

Format your presentation Format the presentation so that it has a professional, consistent look. Applying a design is a relatively easy way of adding a standard format. An even easier approach is to use the Pick a Look Wizard.

Add clip art, graphs, drawings and other objects Use clip art, graphs and drawings to add interest to your presentation and to emphasise specific points.

Complete the presentation Create the speaker's notes and audience handouts to support the presentation. For an autorunning presentation define the presentation parameters, such as the transition time between slides.

Save and print slides, notes, handouts and outline pages If you are working on a large presentation you should save your presentation at regular intervals. Also, you may wish to print slides before you create notes, so that the slides can be checked and used in the creation of the notes. However, ultimately, it is useful to print the complete presentation.

Some tips for effective presentations

This brief section is intended as a reminder that an effective presentation is more than a set of good presentation graphics. PowerPoint cannot create an effective presentation for you. It is only a tool in that process. So, as you develop your presentation graphics with the assistance of PowerPoint it is important to have a view of the total presentation. The key issues are as follows.

Message – No presentation should ever be given if there is not a clear message to communicate. This message might take the form of a series of recommendations, it might be a new insight into an area of knowledge, it might be a report on progress to date. The first step in preparing a presentation is to think about what it is you want to tell your audience. The next step is to consider to whom you wish to convey that message.

Audience – Who is the audience? How many people are in the audience? What is their knowledge and experience of the area of your presentation? How can you keep them interested in what you have to say? What do you want them to do as a result of listening to your presentation? How well do you know your audience? What are their expectations? If you can find out any of this information before you start to prepare your presentation you will feel more comfortable. Above all else, however difficult it may seem, do not be intimidated by your audience. Most people have been in the same position themselves, and however accomplished as presenters they might be now, they had to start somewhere.

Structure and content – Table 1.1 lists some pointers that might be useful to consider:

- What is the main purpose: to motivate, to inform, to change things or to persuade?
- What are the main points that you need to make to get your message across?
- Would it be helpful to give the audience any information in advance?
- Will handouts, or summaries of your paper be useful for the audience?
- How long have you got for your presentation?
- What is an interesting and informative title?
- What level of detail and technical jargon will the audience understand?
- How will you gain the immediate attention of your audience?
- Structure your presentation into three main sections: introduction, middle and conclusion
- Relate your main points together to form a cohesive argument
- Decide when a summary might aid the flow of your presentation
- Consider the visual aids that might assist in illustrating points
- Anticipate the questions that the audience might ask and be prepared to respond
- Reflect on the most effective way to close your presentation.

Table 1.1 : Structure and content of presentations – some pointers

Delivery and style – You need to decide on the delivery mode of the presentation. You will note that, in keeping with good practice, PowerPoint offers facilities for creating slides and then adding speaker's notes. Presentations based on notes are generally less stilted than those where the presenter reads from a text. However, the latter approach lends security and, if it is necessary, ensure that you are very familiar with the text, so that you can speak with appropriate emphasis. A good set of slides can help you to remember the key content of your presentation, and draw out emphases.

Non-verbal communication is also important. Act enthusiastically, make and keep eye contact, smile and look relaxed. Project your voice to the back of the audience, and act confidently. Speak clearly and at conversational speed. Use pauses for emphasis or to indicate breaks between sections, and clearly indicate when you are drawing your presentation to a close with concluding remarks.

Task 2: Structure and content

Consider a presentation that you have recently delivered or are about to deliver.

- What is the message that you wish to deliver?

■ What do you know about the audience?

■ Answer as many of the questions as possible in Table 1.1, in relation to your presentation.

Entering PowerPoint

This activity takes you into PowerPoint so that you can examine the Main PowerPoint Window and investigate Help.

To enter PowerPoint either use Start-Programs and choose Powerpoint, or if you have a shortcut icon on the desktop double-click on it. While the software is loading the pointer will be displayed as an egg timer. PowerPoint will open displaying the Main PowerPoint window. If this is the first time that Powerpoint is used after being installed, the Office Assistant will invite you either to use Help or to start using Powerpoint. You are then invited to choose the type of presentation you wish to create.

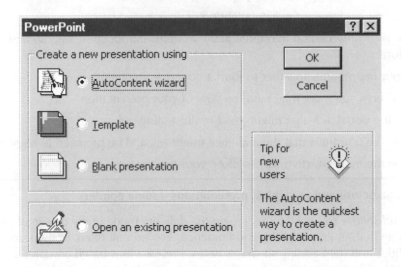

Understanding the main PowerPoint window

The PowerPoint window with its accompanying toolbars and menus closely resembles the window in other Microsoft products, such as Word, Excel and Access. This consistency between Microsoft products should make it relatively easy to become familiar with the basics of PowerPoint. It is worthwhile studying the main window for a moment before trying to make use of it. You will be doing this in Task 3 below. You do not need to remember all the information in the next two pages, but a quick read should serve to orientate you and allow you to make a comparison between PowerPoint and any other Microsoft product with which you are familiar. This section can be used as a ready reference and returned to later as necessary.

The PowerPoint screen can be formatted in a number of different ways and, in particular, it is possible to move and remove toolbars. The screen shown below is the standard PowerPoint main window and these comments relate to this window. Unit 18 discusses the customisation of toolbars.

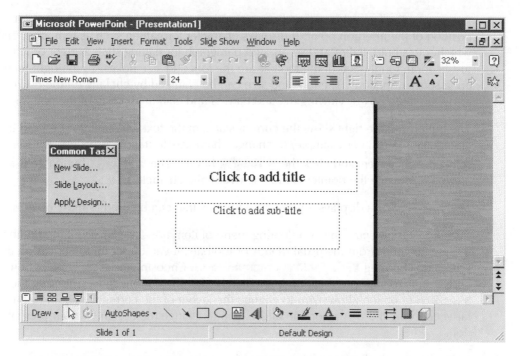

The PowerPoint main window has the following components.

Title bar – shows that you are in Microsoft PowerPoint and the name of the PowerPoint file that you have opened. All PowerPoint files have the extension .ppt however, in Windows 95 extensions are added automatically and Explorer will display a Powerpoint icon next to the filename.

PowerPoint control menu – in the very top left hand corner. If you click on this box a menu with commands for sizing and moving, maximising and minimising the PowerPoint window, and closing PowerPoint is displayed.

Document control menu – in the top left hand corner, but below the PowerPoint control menu. If you click on this box a menu with commands for sizing, moving, and closing the PowerPoint presentation document is displayed.

PowerPoint menu bar – shows the main pull down menus File, Edit, View, Insert, Format, Tools, Slide Show, Window and Help.

Toolbars – Toolbars are useful for quick access to commonly used commands. Clicking on a button on the toolbar activates a command. If you point to a button for a few seconds a small box appears showing the name of the button. These boxes are known as ToolTips. When you first start PowerPoint and open a presentation, the Standard and Formatting toolbars are displayed just below the menu bar, and the Drawing toolbar is displayed at the bottom of the window. Different toolbars appear automatically in each view. These toolbars are listed in Quick Reference 2. You can display and hide toolbars, add buttons to toolbars and otherwise customise toolbars.

Standard Toolbar – includes a number of standard Microsoft buttons such as those which allow you to save presentations, run a spell check, cut and paste, and insert a chart or clip art.

Formatting Toolbar – shows the character and paragraph formatting at the current position of the insertion point. It displays character formatting such as font, size, and whether it is bold, italics and so on, and paragraph formatting such as right or left justification. On the left of the toolbar are the font and size boxes. To the right there are a series of buttons. The font and size can be changed by clicking on the down arrow on these boxes, viewing the alternatives and clicking on one of the options.

The buttons on the right show the current status of the text and can also be used to change that status. For example, to change characters to italic it is necessary to select the characters and click the **Italic** button. The **Italic** button goes in and stays in while the pointer is moving over italic characters.

Drawing Toolbar – displays a number of buttons that can be used to draw objects.

Common Task Menu – this is a floating menu of common tasks to save time finding these commands from the usual menus or toolbars. It can be set up to appear on the screen by choosing View-Toolbar-Common Tasks. Choosing the New Slide option adds a slide to your presentation immediately after the current slide. Choosing the Slide Layout option allows you to change the layout of the current slide, and similarly, choosing the Design option allows you to change the design for your presentation.

Status bar – at the bottom of the screen, shows the status of the system. The status bar tells you the slide that you are working on and, when you choose a command, the status bar displays a short message indicating what that command will do.

Scroll bar – the vertical scroll bar on the right side of the PowerPoint window has an elevator, as well as double arrow buttons, which can be used to move from slide to slide.

Presentation window – displays the presentation on which you are working. At the bottom of the presentation window and above the status bar is a small toolbar showing the **View** buttons that allow you to change easily between the different views available for displaying your presentation.

Task 3: Starting Powerpoint

This task encourages you to familiarise yourself with the PowerPoint screen, and to enter and exit PowerPoint.

1   Start PowerPoint by either using Start-Programs and choosing Powerpoint or, if you have a shortcut icon on the desktop, by double-clicking on it. If this is the first time that Powerpoint has been used then choose Start using Powerpoint. Choose a blank presentation and click on **OK** .

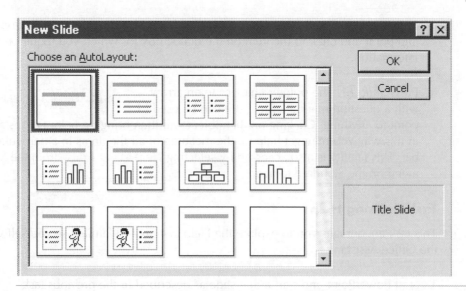

2   Next check that the title slide is selected and click on   **OK** .

3   Move the pointer across the screen until it is over a button on one of the tool-bars. Note the display of the ToolTip naming the button. Move the pointer to another button without clicking to see the description of that button. This also works for the drop-down list boxes in the tool bars.

4   Click on each of the options on the menu bar in turn and observe the range of options on the pull down menus.

5   Identify all the parts of the Powerpoint window according to the description above.

6   Use File-Close to close the presentation document without saving.

7   Use File-Exit to close PowerPoint.

Help

Both Help and examples and demos are available for Powerpoint. There are four main methods of getting into the help system.

1   Pull down the Help menu and select Contents and Index. Choose the **Contents** tab if you are looking for an overview of a particular topic. Choose the **Index** tab to look up a specific item.

2   At any time you can press the *F1* key to get help on whatever you are doing at that moment via the Office Assistant.

3   In many dialog boxes there is a **Help** button on the title bar. Click on this and point and click to the item on the dialog box for which you require extra information.

4   Press *Shift+F1*. The pointer changes to an arrow with a question mark after it and it can be used to point to anything. Clicking on that object will then bring up help. For instance, in this way you may get help on the meaning of all the items in a particular tool bar. This facility is also accessed by selecting Help-What's this? from the Help menu on the Standard toolbar.

? What's This?   Shift+F1

Task 4: Using Help

This task encourages you to explore the Help system and familiarise yourself with the Office Assistant.

1   Start PowerPoint and start a title slide as described in the previous task.

2   Click on the Help menu on the main PowerPoint window. This should cause the pull-down menu to be displayed. Click on Contents and Index to open the Help Topics: Microsoft Powerpoint window.

3   Choose the **Index** tab and enter an item, for example *"printing"* into box 1. Click on **Display**. Choose a topic, click on **Display** and read the help information displayed.

4   When you have finished, close this window by clicking on the cross in the upper right hand corner of the window (if you are not sure where this is consult Quick Reference 1 at the end of this book).

5   Try choosing the **Contents** tab and looking at Working with Slides.

6   Click on the Office Assistant and ask *How do I change the slide layout*, then click on **Search**.

7   You may like to click on Office Assistant's **Option** button and customise your assistant.

   (!) If you choose a different Assistant you will need to load this from the Office CD-ROM.

Creating a new presentation

What you will learn in this unit

There are two ways in which Powerpoint can help you with a presentation. The first is by using the AutoContent Wizard to give you guidelines on how to structure the content of your presentation. You can choose the design that appears on your slides, or select an existing template or create a blank presentation.

By the end of this unit you will be able to:

■ create a presentation using the AutoContent Wizard

■ save, open and close a presentation

■ edit a presentation

■ work with bullet levels

■ run (display on screen) a presentation

■ print an outline of a presentation.

AutoContent Wizard

This activity is about creating a presentation using the AutoContent Wizard. The AutoContent Wizard provides a framework in which to build up your presentation whereby you only need to provide the text that is to appear on the slides. You can choose from a variety of types of presentation, e.g. Selling a Product, Service or an Idea; Recommending a Strategy; Training, Reporting Progress; General; or Communicating Bad News. If none of the structures offered by these types of presentation is appropriate then you would be better to select the Blank Presentation option, which is considered in the next task.

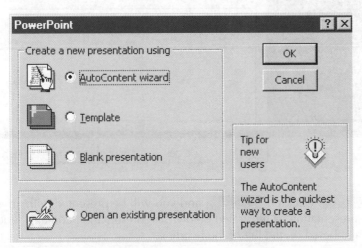

11

The AutoContent Wizard is designed to create a 'ready-made' presentation that requires the minimum amount of work from you. All you need to do is to replace the text in the slides with your own and add slides to the presentation or delete them as required. Once this is complete the presentation can be customised in many ways as illustrated in later units, for example, background design, colour, text enhancement.

Task 1: Creating an AutoContent presentation

In this task we will create a presentation of a project undertaken by a student on a business course. The topic of the project is the refurbishment of a fitness suite at a leisure centre.

1 When you start PowerPoint, the dialog box illustrated on the previous page is displayed. Select the AutoContent Wizard option and click on **OK**. If PowerPoint is already running choose File-New select the **Presentations** tab and choose AutoContent Wizard and click on **OK**.

2 Click on the **Next>** button. In the Next dialog box click on the **General** button and select Generic and click on **Next>**. Select the Presentations, informal meetings, handouts option and click on **Next>**. Choose On-screen Presentation and that you will Produce Handouts. Click on **Next>**.

3 Next enter the presentation title, **Refurbishment of the Fitness Suite at Chelmer Leisure**. Enter your own name in the Your name box.

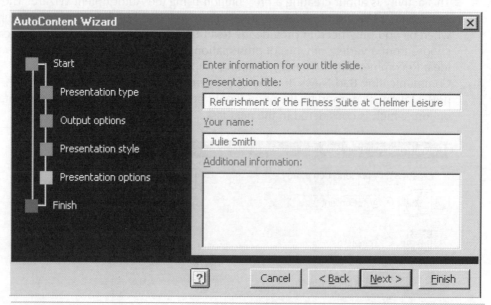

4 Click on **Next>**. Click on **Finish** and you will be presented with an outline view presentation as illustrated below. The presentation contains nine slides, each numbered on the left of the heading.

■ Refurbishment of the Fitness Suite at Chelmer Leisure

Julie Smith

■ Introduction

- State the purpose of the discussion
- Identify yourself

■ Topics of Discussion

- State the main ideas you'll be talking about

■ Topic One

- Detail about this topic
- Supporting information and example
- How it relates to your audience

■ Topic two

- Detail about this topic
- Supporting information and example
- How it relates to your audience

■ Topic Three

- Detail about this topic
- Supporting information and example
- How it relates to your audience

■ Real Life

- Give an example or real life anecdote
- Sympathise with the audience's situation if appropriate

■ What this means

- Add a strong statement that summarises how you feel or think about this topic
- Summarise key points you want your audience to remember

■ Next Steps

- Summarise any actions required of your audience
- Summarise any follow up action items required of you

PowerPoint displays an AutoContent presentation in Outline View. Outline View summarises the text of the slides. The slides may also be viewed in other views as discussed in Unit 3.

Saving, closing and opening a presentation

This activity assumes that you are familiar with the conventions for filenames and are able to choose the desired folder in which to save your presentation. The first time you save a presentation, the Save As dialog box displays, you select the folder in which the file is to be saved and name it. Subsequent saves will take place 'invisibly' as your updated version will overwrite the previous one. If you are able to make backups of your work (e.g. save to a floppy disk) then this is a habit that you should cultivate.

Once you have finished working on a presentation you should close it. All presentations must be closed before you can exit from PowerPoint.

Task 2: Saving, closing and exiting from PowerPoint

1   Now save the presentation as **Project** using File-Save. In the Save in drop down box select the folder in which the presentation is to be saved. Enter the name **Project** in the File name box and save it.

2   Close the presentation using File-Close.

3   Exit from PowerPoint by choosing File-Exit.

Opening and editing a presentation

To open an existing presentation, choose the Open an Existing Presentation option from the main PowerPoint window or use File-Open or click on the **Open** button on the toolbar. Through the Open dialog box select the folder of the file you wish to retrieve and click on the filename and click on **Open** , or alternatively double click on the filename.

Text on the slides may be edited either in Outline View or Slide View. To begin with we shall edit text in Outline View only. Other views will be considered later. Before editing it is usually necessary to select the text concerned. The following table summarises text selection.

To select	Do this
A word	Move the pointer to the word you wish to select and double-click on the left mouse button.
A bullet line (but not the slide title)	Move the pointer to the left of the line in question (it will change shape to a four-arrow symbol) and click.
A slide	Move the pointer over the slide icon to the left of the title of the slide you wish to select and click.
Several slides	Select the first slide using the method above. Holding down the *Shift* key move the pointer to the slide icon of the last slide to be included in the selection and click.
A section of your choice	Move the pointer to the beginning of the section, and drag to highlight the section required.

PowerPoint chooses default styles of fonts for the text that appears on the slides. We shall review the formatting of text in Unit 7 but if you have a basic knowledge of word-processing in Word you will already be familiar with the mechanisms for changing font, size and using bold, italic, etc.

Task 3: Editing a presentation

In this task the AutoContent text will be replaced with the text that is to appear on the slides. You will be using this to carry out tasks during the remainder of this book.

1   Start PowerPoint, choose the Open an Existing Presentation option and open the file **Project**.

2   Selecting, deleting, and entering text in Slide Outline View, amend the presentation to read as shown at the end of this task. Save regularly while creating the text of this presentation, using shortcut key *Ctrl-s*.

3   Edit the text of the bullet points in Slide 2 in any way you choose. In Slide 3 – edit the first bullet point, add additional bullet points by pressing Enter at the end of each point. In Slide 4 edit the title of the slide and the bullet points and add an additional point. In Slides 5 and 6 edit the text of the title and the bullet points. In Slides 7 and 8, edit the bullet points. (The next two tasks will consider deleting and adding slides). Save the presentation.

■ *Refurbishment of the Fitness Suite at Chelmer Leisure*

Julie Smith

■ *Introduction*

- *New Fitness Suite Proposals*
- *Improved Marketability and Community Profile for Chelmer Leisure Centre*

■ *Topics of Discussion*

- *Chelmer Leisure Centre*
- *New Fitness Suite Proposals*
- *Implementing the New Fitness Suite*

■ *Chelmer Leisure Centre*

- *26,313 people in a year*
- *12,596 people participate in Aerobic Activities*
- *2,730 people use the Weight Room*
- *Potential Pool of Users of Improved Fitness Suite*

■ *New Fitness Suite Proposals*

- *Universal Proposal*
- *Atlanta Proposal*
- *Physique Proposal*

■ *Implementing the Fitness Suite*

- *Staff Training*
- *Local Competition*
- *Pricing, Promotion, Market Research*

■ *Summary of Key Points*

- *A new Fitness Suite would improve profitability and contributions to the community*
- *Preferred configuration is that offered by Atlanta*
- *In implementing the new suite attention needs to be paid to staff training and marketing*

■ *Recommendations*

- *New Fitness Suite be acquired through Atlanta*
- *Appropriate staff training is undertaken*
- *Appropriate marketing be undertaken*
- *Impact on profitability be monitored*

Correcting spelling

PowerPoint deals with spelling mistakes in the same way that Word deals with them. Some spelling mistakes, for example, if you transpose the e and o in the word people, will be automatically corrected. Using the Autocorrect facility you can add other spelling mistakes so that they are automatically corrected. If a word is not recognised it is under-lined with a red wavy line and by clicking on the word with the right mouse button, suggested spellings are shown in a short-cut menu. You can still click on the **Spelling** button in the tool bar to check the spellings in the entire presentation.

You can 'turn off' the spell checking as you type or hide the red wavy lines, using Tools-Options, selecting the **Spellings** tab and selecting the desired option in the Check spelling as you type section.

Deleting and adding slides

Whether you create a presentation using the AutoContent or build one up slide by slide, you are likely to wish to modify the content of your presentation. As well as editing text you may wish to delete, add to or change the order of your slides. This activity considers deleting and adding slides.

To delete a slide in Outline View:

- select the slide by clicking on the slide icon by the slide title and choosing Edit-Delete Slide or by pressing the *Delete* key.

To add a slide in Outline View:

- select the slide before the proposed position of the new slide and choose New Slide from the Common Tasks menu. A slide icon appears and the slides that follow are re-numbered.

Task 4 Deleting a slide

The last slide in our presentation as it stands is not required, so

1   Open the presentation **Project** and select Slide 9 (the last slide).

2   Edit-Delete Slide or press the *Delete* key to delete it. Save the presentation.

Task 5 Inserting a new slide

In this task a slide will be added to the presentation. No text will be added until the next activity as the new slide will be used as a means of exploring the different levels of bulleting available.

1   With the presentation **Project** still open select Slide 5 (New Fitness Suite Proposals).

2   Click on New Slide in the Insert menu. (The next task will complete this slide.) Accept the Bulleted list layout.

Bullets and indents

PowerPoint allows you to use more than one level of bulleting, i.e. bullets within bullets. By default each level has a different bullet symbol and each level is progressively smaller in size. The size of the slide and readability of the bullet points will restrict your use of levels of bullets as you should aim to keep slides relatively uncluttered. Bullet symbols may be altered as will be illustrated in Task 7 and the font for each level may also be altered but this will be considered later.

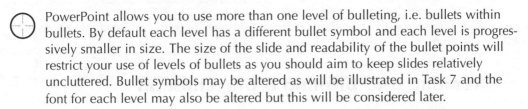

Demotion and promotion of bullet levels is achieved using the Promote and Demote buttons in the vertical tool bar to the left of the screen.

Task 6 Bullet levels

This task continues from the previous one.

1   Add the title ***Preferred Configuration*** in the space next to the new screen icon that has now appeared. Press *Enter* for a new line and another new slide title appears. Click on the Demote button to demote it to a top level bullet point.

2   Add the text ***Atlanta Proposal***. Press *Enter* and demote this line to level two by clicking on the Demote button.

3   Add the text ***reliable maintenance***. Add a new point and demote it, then enter the text compact equipment. Repeat this for another two levels, (there are only five levels of bullet points) adding the text ***back to back positions*** and ***visually appealing***. If you try to demote the last one nothing happens.

4   Experiment using the Demote and Promote buttons on this set of bullet points. When you have finished experimenting, set the last four bullet points to the second level. Save the presentation.

Task 7: Choosing bullet shapes

In this task the selection of different styles of bullet points will be explored. Continue from the last task.

1 Select the four second level bullet points in Slide 6. To do this click in the middle of the text of the first point being selected and drag down to the last point being selected. If you do a 'drag and drop' instead of a selection don't forget to use Edit-Undo.

2 Choose Format-Bullet to display the Bullet dialog box. In this dialog box you may select the font from which you wish to choose your bullet point, the colour of the point and its relative size. You may choose a bullet point of your own preference or you could try a tick symbol from the font Monotype Sorts. Click on the symbol to select it.

3 Click on **OK** and all the bullet points in the selection will be altered. Save the presentation.

4 Experiment with changing bullet points elsewhere in the presentation but do not save these changes.

Running and printing a presentation

Finally having created a presentation you can view the slides on screen (other viewing media will be considered later). You can view the presentation starting at any slide and you can move forwards or backwards through the slides.

So far we have been working in Outline View although you will probably have been aware of a small window displaying the slide in miniature. However, before other views are considered we will print an outline of the presentation. Both running and printing a presentation will be illustrated in the following two tasks.

Task 8: Running a presentation

1 Position the insertion point in Slide 1 and click on the **Slide Show** button ⬚ in the status bar at the bottom of the window.

2 The first slide appears full-screen. To advance a slide either click the mouse button or press *Page Down*. Pressing *Page Up* will cause the previous slide to display. At the end of the slides you are returned to the Outline View.

You can view the presentation from any slide by positioning the insertion point in that slide before clicking on the **Slide Show** button. To return to Outline View at any time press the *Escape* key.

Task 9: Printing an outline of a presentation

1   With the presentation Project still open choose File-Print and in the Print What drop down list box select Outline View.

2   Click on OK and the Outline View of the presentation will be printed.

3   Close the presentation using File-Close.

Understanding PowerPoint views

What you will learn in this unit

You can switch among five views of your presentation, as you create it. This unit explains the role of the different views and the way in which you can move from slide to slide, edit text in each of the different views and sort slides. By the end of this module you will be able to:

- appreciate the functions of the different views
- switch between views
- move from slide to slide in different views
- in Outline View, change the order of the slides, and cut and copy and paste text
- in Slide View, create a new presentation, enter text in placeholders, edit text creating bulleted lists, change the order of the slides, and insert and delete slides.

At the end of this unit you should feel confident to produce basic text based slides, starting with either the AutoContent Wizard or the blank presentation.

Recognising the different views

Each different View gives you a different way of looking at your work and offers different capabilities. Click on the **View** buttons at the bottom left of the PowerPoint window to switch between views, or choose the appropriate option from the View menu.

To move from Outline View to Slide View, ensuring that a specific slide is displayed, double click on the icon for the desired slide in the outline.

The Views are as follows.

Slide View – In Slide View you work on one slide at a time. You can type text, change the slide layout, add graphics, draw shapes, and add artwork and graphics from other applications.

Outline View – In Outline View you work only with slide titles and either the main text, or the full text. The focus is on organising your presentation and developing the basic structure and content.

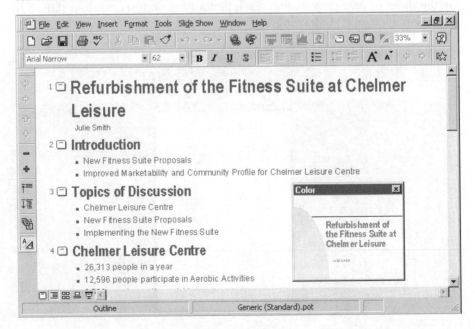

Slide Sorter View – In Slide Sorter View you see a miniature of each slide, complete with graphics and text. Slide Sorter View offers the opportunity to view several of your slides at once, so that you can see how the presentation flows. In Slide Sorter

View, you can reorder slides, add transitions and set the timing for electronic presentations. Slide Sorter View is intended to help you to draw your individual slides into a presentation.

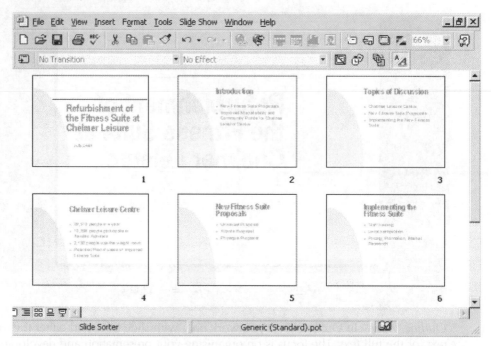

Notes Page View – In Notes Page View you can create speaker's notes for all or any of the slides in your presentation. Each Notes Page corresponds to a slide. Speaker's notes can include text, drawings and other objects.

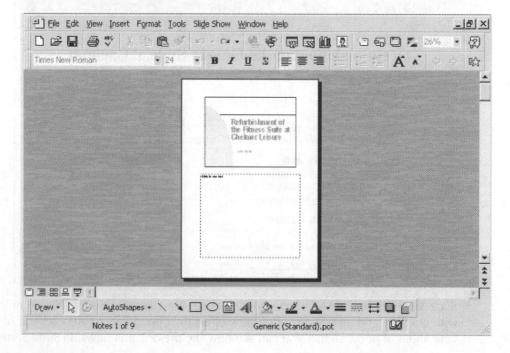

Slide Show View – In Slide Show View you can see your slides as an electronic presentation. Each slide fills the screen in turn, and slides are displayed in sequence, in accordance with the transitions and timing that you set in Slide Sorter View.

Refurbishment of the Fitness Suite at Chelmer Leisure

Julie Smith

Task 1: Investigating the different views

Open the presentation, **Project**, which you created in Unit 2. Using the 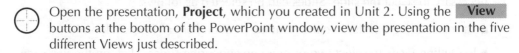 View buttons at the bottom of the PowerPoint window, view the presentation in the five different Views just described.

Moving from slide to slide

Most presentations consist of more than one slide, so it is necessary to move from slide to slide. The procedure for moving from slide to slide is different depending upon the View that you are in:

Slide view – click on the Previous Slide or Next Slide button just below the vertical scroll bar, or drag the box inside the scroll bar until the desired slide number and title are displayed, and then release the mouse button.

Outline View – use the scroll bar to scroll the screen display until the slide that you want to work with is visible. Click on the Slide icon (the icon to the left of the slide's title) to select the slide, or click anywhere inside the text to edit it.

Slide Sorter view – click on the desired slide. A thick border appears around the selected slide. Use the arrow keys or point and click to select a different slide.

Notes Pages View – click on the **Previous Slide** or **Next Slide** button, or drag the box inside the scroll bar until the desired slide is displayed, and then release the mouse button.

Slide Show View – click anywhere on the screen or click the right hand mouse button and select **Next** or **Previous**, or press Page Up or Page Down. To exit press Esc.

Task 2: Moving between slides

Using the presentation, **Project,** which you created in Unit 2, and working in each View in turn, experiment with moving between slides.

Outline View and Slide Sorter View – selecting, and sorting slides and moving text

The work that you did in Unit 2 will have familiarised you with the creation of text in Outline View. This activity introduces two additional features that you might find useful: moving slides and moving text. Although these operations can be performed in other Views, Outline View is a good one to use for this purpose because you have all the text in one scrollable document. Slide Sorter View is also a good View to use for sorting or moving slides.

Outline View and Slide Sorter View – selecting slides

Before you can move a slide you need to be able to select it. In Notes Pages View or Slide View the currently displayed slide is selected, but in Outline View it is necessary to select the slide. Slides can be selected as follows.

- To select a single slide, in either Outline or Slide Sorter View, click on it.
- In Outline View, to select two or more neighbouring slides, click on the first slide and then hold down the Shift key while clicking on the last slide in the group.
- In Slide Sorter View, to select two or more neighbouring or non-neighbouring slides, hold down the Shift key while clicking on each slide. Note that if you wish to remove a highlighted slide from a set of selected slides, click on it while holding down the Shift key.

Outline View – sorting slides

To move a slide from one location to another in Outline View, select the slide, and then drag the title icon from its present position to its new position. As you drag the slide icon a horizontal line appears to make placement easier.

Slide Sorter View – sorting slides

To move a slide in Slide Sorter View, drag the selected slide from its present location to its new location. As you drag the slide, the mouse pointer becomes the drag and drop shape. A vertical line between slides indicates the drop point, which is where the slide will be re-positioned if the mouse button is released.

Outline View – cutting, copying and pasting slides and text

Any text or slides can also be deleted or moved using an appropriate combination of cutting, copying and pasting. First select the slides or text to be changed.

- To cut (remove and place in the clipboard) a slide or piece of text choose Edit-Cut. Don't forget, you can use Edit-Undo if you make a mistake.

- To copy (leave original in place and put a copy in the clipboard) a slide or piece of text choose Edit-Copy, move the insertion point to where the text or slide should be inserted and choose Edit-Paste.

- To move a slide or piece of text choose Edit-Cut, move the insertion point to where the text or slide should be inserted and choose Edit-Paste. However, to move slides it is much easier to use one of the methods described above.

- To move small selections of text it is quicker to use the 'drag and drop' method. Select the text, point to the selection and drag the dotted insertion point to the intended new position and release the mouse button. Don't forget there is Edit-Undo if you make a mistake.

Task 3: Slide sorting and copy and paste

Use the presentation **Project**.

1 View the presentation in Slide Sorter View. Follow the instructions above and move one of the slides to a different position in the presentation. Now, just to check that you can move slides successfully, move it back again!

2 Change to Outline View. Select a section of text and using Edit-Copy, copy the text to the clipboard. Then move the insertion pointer to the position where you would like to insert the text and use Edit-Paste. The text should appear in its new position. To remove this duplicate text, select it and press *Delete*.

3 Continuing in Outline View, select a section of text and drag it to another position. Use Edit-Undo to undo your move. It is not necessary to save these changes.

4 Exit the presentation by using File-Close.

Using blank presentations and templates

What you will learn in this unit

Slide View is useful for editing all of the objects on a slide, including text, graphics and other objects. Some of these objects are not displayed in Outline View. The AutoContent Wizard is useful if you are planning a lengthy presentation but for small presentations or presentations that do not fit any of the models offered by the Wizard you can either choose a blank presentation or one based on a template.

By the end of this module you will be able to:

- create a presentation starting with a blank presentation
- create a presentation using a template
- add and delete slides
- apply a design template.

Starting with a blank presentation

To create a new presentation if PowerPoint is already running, choose File-New and with Blank Presentation highlighted, under the General tab, click on OK. If you have just started Powerpoint select the Blank Presentation option in the PowerPoint Main dialog box. PowerPoint will then display the New Slide dialog box from which you can choose the type of slide layout you require. Once you have selected the type of slide you want a blank slide will be displayed in Slide View.

The most common objects on a slide are text objects; these are introduced here and further explored in later units. All objects have to be selected by clicking on them. So, to edit a text object, click on the object to select it and then click to position the insertion point in the text at the position where you wish to undertake some editing. In the next task you will use Slide View to create a new presentation without the aid of the AutoContent Wizard. Note that you can switch to Outline View or any of the other Views at any time while creating or editing a presentation.

There are a few terms that are useful to introduce at this point.

AutoLayout – the Autolayouts are the slide layouts that are available when you add a new slide to a presentation. AutoLayouts contain ready-made placeholders for titles, text and objects such as clip art graphs and charts. The next unit will begin to look at the AutoLayouts in more detail.

Title placeholder – the title box. To enter the title of the slide click in the place-holder and type in the slide title. This is a component of nearly all the types of slide layout.

Text placeholder – the box into which text can be entered. Click in the text place-holder and type in the text for the slide. Most of the slide layouts have a text place-holder.

Object placeholder – the box into which objects can be placed. Different types of object placeholder cater for text, graphs, tables, organisational charts and clip art. Click to add text in a placeholder or double click to add the specified object. These are available in specific slide layouts.

Task 1: Creating a presentation based on the blank presentation

In this task a new presentation will be created which is based on a blank presenta-tion. It will comprise a title slide and a bullet list slide, which will be added to in subsequent units.

1   If you have just started PowerPoint choose Blank Presentation from the Main dialog box. If PowerPoint is already running choose File-New and with Blank Presentation highlighted click on **OK** .

2   Next select a Title Slide Layout from the AutoLayout dialog box and click on **OK** . Click where it says Click to add title and add the title of the slide: ***Chelmer Estates Chelmer Branch Monthly Briefing***. Click where it says Click to add sub-title and add the sub-title of the slide: ***January 1999 James Copeland***.

3   Click on New Slide in the Insert menu. Choose a bulleted list layout. Add the title ***Overview*** to the slide and then add the following bullet points:

■ ***Good news on sales***

■ ***New branch opens***

■ ***Computer Training***

■ ***Investors in People***

■ ***Enhanced Appraisal Scheme***

4   Save the presentation as **Briefing** and close it.

Starting with a template

PowerPoint offers a number of slide design templates. If you create a presentation using the AutoContent Wizard, a design template is selected for you depending on the type of presentation you have chosen. You can change this later if you wish. If you want to apply a design without using the AutoContent Wizard, then you can base your presentation on a template design as described below. A design can be applied at any time as described in the section on applying a design at the end of this unit.

Task 2: Creating a presentation based on a template

In this task a new presentation will be created which is based on a template. It will comprise a small series of four slides to display the text shown below. For this task only enter the text for Slides 1, 3 and 4 omitting Slide 2. In the next task we will add Slide 2.

We will later use these slides to create an autorunning presentation that might be displayed near the entrance to the leisure centre and used to draw attention to the facilities in the new Fitness Suite. Each slide is composed of a title and accompanying text in a variety of formats.

1   If you have just started PowerPoint choose Template from the Main dialog box. If PowerPoint is already running choose File-New. Select the **Presentation Designs Templates** tab and choose the Ribbons template. The New Slide dialog box will appear.

2   Next select a Bulleted List Layout and click on **OK** Click where it says Click to add title and add the title of the slide (see Slide 1 below). Add the bulleted text in the same way.

Slide 1   **New Fitness Suite**

- *Do you need to fight the flab?*
- *Have you always meant to get fit?*
- *Turn your good resolutions into reality*
- *Try some of our classes in our Fitness Suite*

3   To create the next slide (Slide 3 below) click on New Slide in the Insert menu. Choose a bulleted list layout. Add the title. Remove the bullet points (click on the **Bullet** button in the toolbar) and use a *Tab* to separate the two columns. Don't worry if the look of this slide is not quite right as this will be dealt with in Unit 8.

Slide 3   **Fitness Suite Opening Times**

Monday-Friday	*8.00am to 9.00pm*
Saturday-Sunday	*9.00am to 5.00pm*

4   Add another new slide, Slide 4 shown below, as the third slide in this presentation. Again choose a bulleted list layout and remove the bullets. Use a *Tab* to separate the prices from the time periods. Again don't worry if this slide doesn't look quite right.

Slide 4   **Fitness Suite Passcards**

Why not treat yourself or a friend to a Fitness Suite Passcard?
Gold Pass Cards cost only:

3 month	*£85*
6 month	*£150*
12 month	*£275*

5   Save your presentation as **Advert**.

Slide View – adding and deleting slides

To insert a new slide into a presentation between existing slides, first display the slide after which you wish to add the new slide and either choose Insert-New Slide, or click on the **New Slide** button in the toolbar, or choose New Slide from the Common Tasks menu. If the Common Tasks menu is not visible use View-Toolbars Common Tasks to display it.

To delete a slide, in Slide View or Notes View choose Edit-Delete Slide.

Task 3: Adding a slide to an existing presentation

In this task Slide 2 of the presentation **Advert** will be added.

1 Open the presentation **Advert** in Slide View. Display the first slide and click on New Slide in the Common Tasks menu. Select a bulleted list layout.

2 Add the title as illustrated in Slide 2 below. Click on the frame around the bullet point area and take off the bullets by clicking on the **Bullet** button in the tool bar. Type **Step** and press the _Tab_ key before keying **A good way....** Repeat for the other two points and then type the final sentence in normally. You will observe that your slide is probably rather untidy and doesn't look set out like the example. Don't worry, leave it untidy: when text boxes are introduced in Unit 9 you will see how to control text layout.

Slide 2   ***Aerobics Open Day***

       Step   ***A good way to start your fitness programme***

       Cycle ***Tone up those flabby thighs and strengthen those backs***

       Row   ***Try your hand at our computer-controlled rowing machine***

       Our fitness advisors will be on hand to advise you on a suitable fitness programme

3 Save the presentation **Advert**. Select the first slide and click on the **Slide Show** button to run your slide show. You will see that it is in black and white; the next unit will consider slide looks and layouts.

4 Close the presentation.

Applying a design

A design can be applied to an existing presentation or used in advance of the creation of a presentation. If you use the AutoContent Wizard a design will be applied. This should have happened for the presentation **Project**. If a blank presentation is chosen this is plain and you are very likely to want to change it. The latest version of PowerPoint offers a range of designs to choose from (but not as many as in previous versions) and these can be customised to suit the type of presentation you are creating. Later, we will see how to control colour so that you can customise the presentation according to whether it will be made into black and white overheads, colour overheads, 35mm slides or if it is intended for direct projection or on-screen use.

Task 4: Applying a design

1   Open the presentation **Briefing**. Choose Apply Design from the Common Tasks menu.

2   Select the design entitled Notebook and click on **Apply** . View the slides in Slide View noticing that this design has different bullet points.

3   Use Edit-Undo-Apply Design to return to the default design. Experiment with choosing from some of the other designs and see how the slides look. After each choice use Edit-Undo to return to the default design.

4   Close the presentation without saving any changes.

Applying looks and layouts; using masters

What you will learn in this unit

PowerPoint has a number of facilities that help you to give your presentation a professional appearance. There are two main items that need to be formatted.

- The presentation as a whole – the look of the presentation is controlled through choosing slide designs and by customising slide masters. Using the Apply Design option from the Common Tasks menu a slide design can be chosen. Further customising using the Slide Master will be considered later.

- The individual slides – the layout or structure of individual slides is controlled through its layout. AutoLayout offers you a number of standard layouts from which you can choose.

The formatting for the title and text that is applied by using a template is stored in the master. Every template has a master. So far we have used PowerPoint's supplied templates. Now we investigate the formatting of a new master or the modification of an existing master to create a new template. We shall focus on the Slide Master, which is the master that holds the format for the title and text for slides. Later we shall briefly consider the Notes Master, the Outline Master and the Handout Master.

By the end of this unit you will be able to:

- apply slide layouts
- select a slide design
- appreciate the components of the Slide Master
- be able to change the Slide Master
- be able to make a slide that differs from the Slide Master
- reapply features of the Slide Master to a slide
- print slides.

Using AutoLayout

AutoLayouts allow you to set the structure of a single slide in a presentation. For example, if you want a graph or a picture on a slide then you can choose an AutoLayout that positions the two items for you.

Normally, as you add new slides you select a layout for each slide. If you want to alter the slide layout you can do this as follows.

1   In Slide View, display the slide whose layout you want to set.

2   Choose Format-Slide Layout. The Slide Layout box will appear. Click on the desired layout and click on   Apply .

31

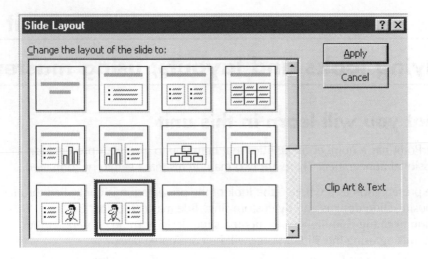

Task 1: Reapplying a layout

1 Open the presentation **Project** that you created in Unit 2. Change to Slide View.

2 Display the slide showing the list of features of the **Atlanta** proposal. Add the following text to the list. (You may have selected different bullet points for this slide in Unit 2.)

- *Robust and safe*

- *Quiet*

- *Easy to use*

- *Range of difficulty levels*

- *Show site discount*

- *Interior design (at additional cost)*

3 You will note that not all the list fits onto the slide, so some re-formatting would be helpful.

4 Choose Slide Layout from the Common Tasks menu, and in the dialog box click on the Layout that shows two parallel bulleted lists. Click on **Apply**.

5 Select the text of the last four points, use Edit-Cut, click in the second column box and use Edit-Paste (you can drag and drop if you wish). Now move the second column box down slightly by dragging its edge so that the points line up with those in the first box.

6 Save the presentation.

Understanding the Title and Slide Masters

The Title Master holds the formatted placeholders for the text on the title slide, together with any background items that appear on this slide. If you create a presentation that does not have a title slide then the Title Master will not be available. The Slide Master holds the formatted placeholders for the title and text, together with any background items that appear on the following slides. Any changes that are made to the Title Master affect only the title slide and changes made to the Slide Master affect all the rest of the slides in your presentation. Both the Title and Slide Masters have three basic components.

Master title (title area for AutoLayouts) – this is the formatted placeholder for slide titles on both the Title and Slide Master. This is where you set the font, colour, size, and alignment of slide titles (as well as title attributes Fill, Line, Shadow), shape and placement on the slide.

Master sub-title or Master text (Object area for AutoLayouts) – this is the formatted placeholder for the sub-title on the Title Master or the main slide text on the Slide Master. This is where you set the font, colour, size, line spacing and alignment of the sub-title or main text as well as the text's attributes (Fill, Line, and Shadow), shape and placement on the slide.

Background items – these are those items that you add to the Title and Slide Master so that they will appear on all the slides in a presentation. Background items typically include art (such as a logo), the date, the time, the page or slide number, and the name of the presentation.

 Text that you type into the text placeholders will not appear on your slides. If you want text to appear on the slides, create a new text box on the Slide Master, using the ▊ Text ▊ tool on the Drawing toolbar. Then type in your text.

Changing a Slide Master

Change a Slide Master as follows.

1 Choose View-Master, and then choose Slide Master.

2 The Slide Master appears. Work with the text font on the Slide Master just as you would on any other slide. Text attributes, such as placement on the slide, font and background items can be changed. Background items will be considered in later units.

3 When you have completed your changes choose View-Slide or click on the ▊ Slide View ▊ button. Examine the slides in the presentation to note that the changes have been applied to the title and all following slides. Check that all slides are satisfactory under the new formatting.

Task 2: Working with the Slide Master

Open the presentation **Advert**. This presentation does not have a title slide so only the Slide Master will be available.

33

1 Choose View-Master, and then choose Slide Master

2 Change the following characteristics of the Slide Master: click on the Title area, and using the Font and Size drop down list boxes on the toolbar, select Bookman Old Style 36pt (if you do not have this font then make a choice from those available to you).

3 When you have completed your changes choose View-Slide. Examine all the slides. Save the presentation **Advert**.

To look at other modifications we will make a copy of this presentation.

4 Use File-Save As and save a copy of this presentation as **Advert1**.

5 Choose View-Master, and then choose Slide Master.

6 Click on the first level in the object area. Edit the bullet style using Format-Bullet and select a different bullet, say, ✱ from the Monotype sorts font. Alter the size of the first level text to 36pt.

7 Click on ▐ **OK** ▌ to view the result. The text size may be a little large for the **Aerobics Open Day** slide. Select this text and change its size to 28pt. This illustrates that you can override master formatting on individual slides (see below).

8 Save and close the presentation **Advert1**. You should now have two different versions of this presentation.

Task 3: Working with the Title Master

If you create a blank presentation, even if it starts with a title slide, it will not have a Title Master. If a Title Master is required one can be added as illustrated in the following task. If you use a design template a Title Master will be available if you include a title slide in your presentation.

1 Open the presentation **Briefing** in Slide View. Choose View-Master-Slide-Master (notice that Title Master is not available). Next choose Insert-New Title Master and a Title Master will be displayed.

2 As with the Slide Master, try altering the fonts in the title and sub-title areas.

3 Make some changes to the styles in the Slide Master which are different and view the result. Select some fonts that you think would be suitable for this presentation and save it.

Tips on using Title and Slide Masters

1 Consider using the Drawing toolbar to add a border. A border frames text and graphics.

2 Experiment with border designs. Try changing the line style to make the border look more stylish or experiment with the adjustment handle to create decorative effect in the corners of the border.

3 When you add background items to the Title and Slide Master, the title and text always appear on top of the background items on your slides.

4 If you delete the title or text placeholders, they can be restored by choosing Format-Slide Layout and clicking on the **Reapply** button.

5 Insert the date, time and page numbers on the masters.

Making a slide that differs from the Slide Master

Not all slides need to follow the Slide Master. For example, it may be useful to change the background colour of one or two slides in order to emphasise or differentiate the slides.

Make a slide that differs from the Slide Master as follows.

1 Display the slide that you want to change. Make any changes to the font size and colour, background colours and the colour scheme.

2 Any changes will not affect the other slides.

 Although you can change a slide so that it differs from the Slide Master, you cannot apply a design to an individual slide.

Task 4: Making a slide that differs from the Slide Master

In this task a different font for the slide titles will be added to the Slide Master of the presentation **Advert1**. This font will be changed in the title of the first slide.

1 Open the presentation **Advert1**. Choose View-Master and select Slide Master.

2 Click on Click to edit Master Title style. Choose a different font and alter the application of bold, italic and shadow.

3 View the slides. Save the presentation.

4 Move to the first slide in Slide View. Select the title text. Choose a different font, for example, a larger size. Alter bold, italic and shadow.

5 View the slides and save the presentation.

Reapplying Slide Master characteristics

If you have experimented with a slide, you may choose to re-apply the Slide Master characteristics.

Reapply the Master Title and text formats to a slide as follows.

1 Display the slide to which you wish to reapply the Slide Master.

2 Choose Format-Slide Layout. The Slide Layout dialog box appears with the current slide's layout selected.

3 Choose Reapply . Check that the text and placeholders on the slide now conform to the Slide Master.

Task 5: Reapplying Slide Master characteristics

1 Continue working with the presentation **Advert1**. Select the first slide in Slide View.

2 Choose Format-Slide Layout. Choose Reapply . Check that the text and place-holders on the slide now conform to the Slide Master.

3 Save the presentation.

Printing slides

The first step in producing printed copies of your presentation is to check the current slide setup. The slide setup determines the size and orientation of the slides when printed or converted into 35mm format. Normally the default setting need not be changed. The settings can be viewed using File-Page Setup to display the Page Setup dialog box. You may wish to alter the orientation of the way slides or notes, handouts and outlines are printed.

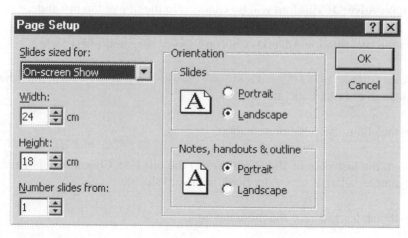

Slides may be printed by selecting Slides from the Print What list box in the Print dialog box. You can choose whether to print all the slides, the current slide or a selection of slides. To make a selection of slides list the slide numbers in the Slides box. For example, if you wish to print Slides 1 to 5 inclusive and Slide 8 then you would type *1-5,8* in the Slides box.

Alternatively, before using File-Print display your presentation in Slide Sorter or Outline View and select the slides you wish to be printed. To select more than one slide hold down the *Shift* key. Choose the Selection option in the Print dialog box. The Copies box will let you print multiple copies.

Print options in the Print dialog box

Print to File	Instead of printing, an output file is created on disk. This may be transferred to another computer and printed using its printer.
Print Hidden Slides	Hidden slides are discussed in Unit 18. This option will print slides that have been hidden using the Tools-Hide Slide command.
Scale to Fit Paper	Scales the slides to fit the printed page even if the slides have been set up for a different page size.
Pure Black and White	Allows colour slides to be printed properly on a black and white printer. It replaces colour with black and white patterns. Printing may be faster but there may be some loss of formatting.
Frame slides	Adds a thin border around the edge of printouts of slides, notes and handouts.

Task 6: Printing slides

In this task a selected set of slides from the presentation **Advert** will be printed in black and white.

1   Open the presentation **Advert** in Slide Sorter View and select the first and the last slides.

---

2   Choose File-Print.

---

3   Choose the Selection option, check the Black and White option and click on
     OK to print.

Working with notes and handouts

What you will learn in this unit

While, in an autorunning presentation, the slides need to convey the complete message, most slide presentations are used to draw attention to key points in a presentation that are being offered by a speaker. In preparing for such presentations most speakers will wish to prepare slides, handouts and notes (for themselves), in parallel. PowerPoint makes this process very straightforward since notes and hand-outs can be generated automatically from the slides. These notes and handouts can then be further customised. Each slide in a presentation has an accompanying notes page, which includes a smaller version of the slide along with room for notes, as discussed in Unit 3. Printed notes are a useful reminder for the speaker.

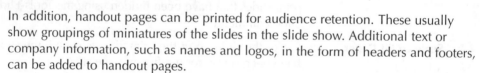

In addition, handout pages can be printed for audience retention. These usually show groupings of miniatures of the slides in the slide show. Additional text or company information, such as names and logos, in the form of headers and footers, can be added to handout pages.

You may wish to take notes during a presentation, possibly to make a record of comments made by the audience, or to note an action plan resulting from discussion during the presentation. Notes pages can be accessed on screen during the presentation for note recording by using the Meeting Minder, a facility provided by PowerPoint.

Notes and Handout Masters perform the same functions for notes and handouts that the Slide Master performs for slides. These masters contain all the information for layout and background in these contexts. By the end of this unit you will be able to

■ add notes to notes pages

■ work with Notes and Handout Masters

■ print notes and handouts

■ use the Meeting Minder to take notes during a presentation.

Creating notes

You can key in notes to remind yourself of the points that you are going to explain while the slide is being viewed. In Notes View simply key in your notes. You can then print your notes for use during your presentation. You can make Notes Pages for as many slides as you want and type your script on the Notes Pages to accompany your presentation. If you want to provide pages on which your audience can make notes, then print Notes Pages but leave the notes area blank. The layout and formatting of Notes Pages may be altered and the Notes Master can be used to apply such changes throughout all the Notes Pages associated with a presentation.

The Notes Master can be used to:

1 add a picture, such as a company logo, that will appear on each Notes Page

2 move and resize the Notes Page objects such as the areas for dates, page numbers, headers and footers

3 choose a colour scheme or background for the Notes Pages (which affects only the Notes Page, and not the presentation itself)

4 set up the Body Area to control the general layout and formatting of the text in the notes area of each Notes Page.

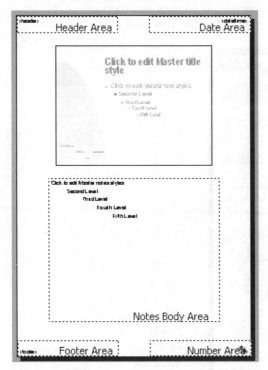

To display the Notes Master choose View-Master and select Notes Master. To add date, page number, header and footer placeholders, as illustrated above, choose Format-Notes Master Layout and tick the placeholders you require.

Change any of the elements of the Master that you wish to.

Creating handouts

Handout pages can contain two, three or six slides per page. Space can be left on handouts if you want the audience to be able to take notes. Alternatively, you may add some text of your own. Handout Masters can be accessed and modified in a similar way to the Slide and Notes Masters. Headers and footers, date and page number placeholders can be added as for the Notes Master (see below for more details). The Handout Master can be used to add art and text to your handouts. Typically you might wish to add the title of the presentation and a logo.

To display the Handout Master choose View-Master and then select Handout Master. Change any elements of the master that you wish to.

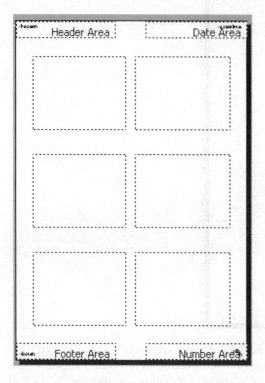

Outline master

Although there isn't a separate 'outline master', you can set headers and footers for printing with outlines in the same way as for handouts. If you set headers or footers for either outlines or handouts they will be common to both outlines and handouts.

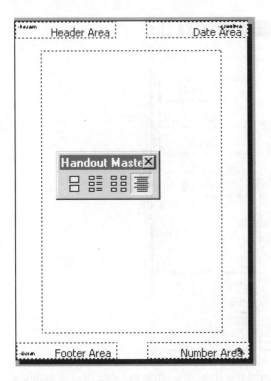

Adding dates, page numbers, headers and footers

Dates and page numbers are added as headers or footers. Other information such as the company name, logo or title of the event (e.g. conference or seminar) can be added to the header or footer. Through Format-Master you can add placeholders to the Notes and Handout Masters. The headers and footers in notes and handouts can be different from those in Title and Slide Masters. Headers and footers can be altered on individual slides but not on individual notes, handouts or outline pages. Headers and footers are the same on the Notes, Handout and Outline pages.

After you add information to the header or footer, you can change the format or position of the header and footer on your notes pages, handouts, and outlines by changing them on their corresponding masters.

Add date, time or page numbers to slides, notes and handouts as follows.

1 Choose View-Header Footer. If you are working with slides click on the **Slide** tab and if you are working with either Notes or Handouts click on the **Notes and Handouts** tab.

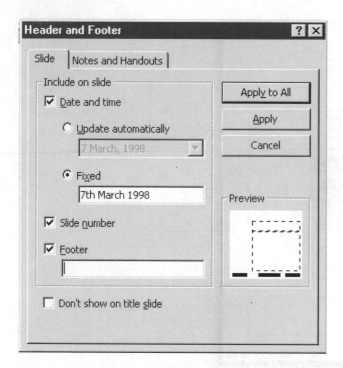

2 For slides, choose whether to add the date, the slide number and possibly a footer. You may add a fixed date or allow the current date to be added. You can apply these settings to all the slides by clicking on the **Apply to All** button or you can apply them to the slide you are working with by clicking on the **Apply** button. If you don't want the date, slide number or footer to appear on the title slide then check the Don't show on title slide check box.

3 For notes, handouts and outlines, the procedure is the same as for slides, except that a header is available and headers and footers apply to all pages.

Task 1: Working with the Notes Master

Open the presentation **Project**. Choose View-Master and then select Notes Master. Perform the following changes on the Notes Master.

1 Change the size of the Notes area by selecting it and dragging, say, the middle handle of the lower edge, upwards.

2 Still in the Notes area, click in the level 1 text (Click to edit Master text styles) and make it larger by clicking on the **Increase Font Size** button on the toolbar. Apply full justification using Format-Alignment-Justify.

3 Click in the level 2 text and make it italic and apply bullets by clicking on the **Bullet** button in the toolbar. If the ruler is not visible, use View-Ruler to display the ruler and set a hanging indent by dragging the indent margin triangle (the upper triangle of the second set of margin markers) a small distance to the left. Apply full justification.

4   Return to the presentation and display it in Notes Pages View.

5   Select Slide 4 (Notes 4, entitled **Chelmer Leisure Centre**). Click in the notes area and type in the following text. Check that the text is formatted in a way that you would wish.

These statistics relate to 1997

■ *number of people is actual*

■ *Aerobic and Weight Room use extrapolated from a 3 month survey, June to September*

6   Use View-Header Footer, select the ▐ Notes and Handouts ▐ tab, and choose to add a date that updates automatically and click on ▐ **Apply to All** ▐ .

7   Save the presentation.

Task 2: Working with the Handout Master

Continue to work with the presentation **Project.** Choose View-Master and then select Handout Master.

1   Click on the second option (Show positioning of 3-per-page handouts) in the Handout Master toolbar.

2   To add date, page number, header and footer placeholders choose Format-Handout Master Layout and tick all the placeholders.

3   Using View-Header Footer, add a header that reads *Chelmer Leisure* and a footer that reads *Fitness Suite Proposals*. To see the effect we will print a notes page in the next task.

4   Save the presentation.

Printing notes, handouts and outlines

Both Notes and Handout pages print in portrait orientation. If you wish to change this then use the options in the Page setup dialog box.

To print speaker's notes, choose File-Print and select Notes Pages from the Print What list box. If you only want to print the slides that have notes then choose the Slides option in the Print Range section and list the slide numbers that you want printed.

Handouts may be printed by selecting Handouts from the Print What list box in the Print dialog box. Handouts may be printed as two, three or six slides per page. The three slides per page handouts leave room for the audience to take notes. A presentation outline may be printed by selecting Outline View from the Print What list box in the Print dialog box.

You should next consider the type of printer you are using, including whether it prints in colour or black only. You can choose appropriate print options as detailed at the end of Unit 5.

Task 3: Printing notes and handouts

1   Continuing from the last two tasks, to print the notes entered on Slide 4, choose File-Print and select Notes Pages. Click on the Slides option and enter **4** and click on OK .

2   Now print handouts by choosing File-Print and selecting Handouts (three slides per page). Click on OK . If you want to print one page to check the headers and footers then in the Slides section enter *1-3*.

3   Click on Slide View to return to Slide View.

Meeting Minder

The Meeting Minder allows you can take minutes or add notes during a computer generated slide show. If you take notes during a presentation, the Meeting Minder dialog box appears only on your screen; your audience sees only the slide show. Take notes or minutes during a slide show as follows.

1   Make sure that you are in Slide Show View.

2   Click on the right mouse button and choose Meeting Minder or Speakers Notes.

3   If you have chosen Speakers Notes a box appears in which you can add or edit the notes for that slide. To finish click on Close .

4   If you have chosen Meeting Minder a box appears in which you can add or edit any notes taken during the presentation. Click in the box, type your minutes, and then click on OK . There is also the provision to record actions that result from discussions; action items will appear on a slide at the end of the presentation.

5   If you want to print the minutes you can export them to Word by choosing the Meeting Minutes tab, in the Meeting Minder dialog box, and clicking on the Export button. Select the Send meeting minutes and action items to Microsoft Word check box, and then click Export Now . Word opens a new document that contains your minutes, which you can print.

Formatting and checking text

What you will learn in this unit

It is important that the text on slides is accurate and appropriately formatted. Text on slides can be formatted to be consistent across a presentation using the Slide Master, or formatted on individual slides. Here we will work with formatting text on individual slides. Many of the skills that you will learn in this unit can be applied when formatting text in slides, handouts and notes. By the end of this unit you will be able to:

■ check your text using the Spelling checker

■ find and replace text

■ apply type fonts

■ apply type faces

■ apply alignment

■ apply line spacing

■ insert dates and slide numbers.

If you are familiar with Word you will note that these operations are performed in PowerPoint in a very similar way to the way in which they are performed in Word. You may like to focus solely on the tasks in this unit, if this is the case.

Checking spelling

PowerPoint checks spelling interactively, by default, as you type, as we have seen in Unit 2. You can remove spell checking as you type using Tools-Options, selecting the **Spelling** tab and removing the tick from the Spelling check box. For completeness the spellchecker is discussed here.

The Spelling checker checks the entire presentation including all slides, notes, and Handout Pages and Master Views. Even with spelling checked as you type it is good practice to check your spelling just as you finalise your presentation, but you may also want to run a spelling check once you have completed the text for the slides.

To check spelling and any typos, choose Tools-Spelling, or click on the **Spelling** button. The Spelling dialog box appears.

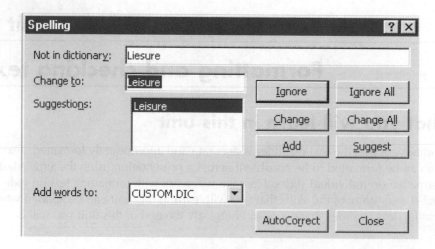

When the spelling checker comes across a word that it does not recognise it shows it in the Not in Dictionary box. In the Change To box the spelling checker offers a correction. If there is more than one possible correction these are listed in the Suggestions box. Behind the Spelling dialog box the document can be seen with the word in question highlighted.

There are a number of options available, shown by the buttons.

1   If the Change To box contains the correct spelling click on the **Change** button

2   If the correct spelling is in the Suggestions box click on it to put it into the Change To box and click on the **Change** button.

3   If you think that the mistake may be repeated throughout the presentation then use the Change All button instead of the Change button.

4   If the word is correct but it is not in the spelling checker's dictionary then choose **Ignore**, or you may **Add** the word to your own dictionary. Consult the help files or manual for information about creating your own dictionary. Use **Ignore All** to ignore all occurrences of the word throughout the presentation.

PowerPoint will indicate when the spellcheck is complete.

Finding and replacing text

If you used a word or phrase and cannot remember which slide you used it on you can use Find to locate that word or phrase. On the other hand if you want to replace one word with another, Replace will locate the offending word and offer options for replacing the word or phrase. This may be particularly useful if you need to replace a word that has a number of occurrences throughout your presentation. Suppose for instance you are updating an old presentation and the company name has changed. Replace can be used to find all occurrences of the old name, and replace it with the new name.

Replacing text

Replace text as follows.

1 Choose Edit-Replace. The Replace dialog box appears.

2 In the Find What box enter the text string to be located.

3 In the Replace With box enter the replacement string.

You may then optionally select either or both of the following options.

1 Match Case finds text that matches the capitalisation in the Find What text box.

2 Find Whole Word Only skips any occurrences of the text that are part of another word.

Once the search string has been found there are three replacement options available.

1 To replace the search string with the replacement string, click on the **Replace** button.

2 To skip to the next occurrence of the search string without replacing it click on the **Find Next** button.

3 To replace all occurrences of the search string with the replace string click on **Replace All** .

The **Replace All** option should be used with extreme caution. Unintentional replacements may occur especially if the search string forms part of other words.

Finding Text

Finding text is similar to replacing text, without the replace elements.

You may find a text string as follows.

1 Choose Edit-Find to summon the Find dialog box.

2 In the Find What box enter the text string to be located.

3 Press *Enter* and click on the **Find Next** button to find the next occurrence of the text string.

4 To move to the next occurrence click on the **Find Next** button again.

Task 1: Find and replace

1 Open the presentation **Project**.

2 Find all occurrences of the following words: Leisure, Fitness, Centre, Aerobics, Activity.

3   Replace Atlanta with **Universal**. Undo this replacement.

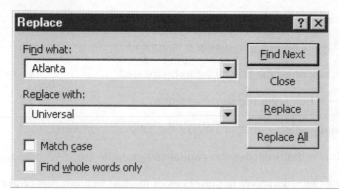

Formatting text with the Formatting toolbar

The Formatting toolbar, as shown below, contains a number of boxes and buttons to assist in formatting text.

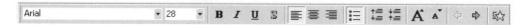

To change the appearance of text, the text must first be selected. Then clicking on the appropriate button or down arrow offers the following options.

1   To change fonts, click on the arrow to the right of the Font list, and then click on the desired font.

2   To specify a different type size, click inside the Font Size text box and type a size, or click on the arrow to the right of the text box and select a size.

3   A quicker way to increase or decrease the text size is to use the **Increase Font Size** or **Decrease Font Size** button.

4   To add a style or effect to the text, such as bold, italic, underline, and/or shadow, click on the appropriate button.

5   To add alignment, click on one of the alignment buttons.

6   To insert bullets, click on the **Bullet** button.

7   To increase or decrease paragraph spacing, click on the appropriate paragraph spacing button.

Task 2: Using fonts

Create a new presentation with the following three slides. Save it as **Facility**.

Slide 1 (title)   ***Chelmer Leisure***

                       • ***Fitness Suite and Multi-Gym***

Slide 2 (bullet)   ***Fitness Suite Facilities***
- ***Sunbeds***
- ***Sauna and Steam Room***
- ***Jacuzzi relaxation lounge***
- ***Satellite TV***

Slide 3 (bullet)   ***Multi-Gym Facilities***
- ***Super Circuit Training***
- ***Cardio-vascular equipment***
- ***Fitness Testing***
- ***Computerised video screen***
- ***Fully air conditioned***

1   Display the second slide in Slide View. Select the title and make it bold. Select individual words or points and experiment with bold, italic, underlining and shadow effects.

2   Display the third slide in Slide View. Select individual words or points and experiment with different fonts. Investigate the effect of the `Increase` and `Decrease Font Size` buttons.

3   Save and view the presentation. Make further changes if you wish.

Using the Font dialog box

The Font dialog box is another way of formatting text, which offers a wider range of text enhancements.

Use the Font dialog box as follows.

1   Select the text to be formatted.

2   Choose Format-Font, and the Font dialog box appears.

3   From this dialog box, select a font, font style and size by clicking on the appropriate entry.

4   In the Effects box, select any special effects you want to add to the text, such as Underline, Shadow or Emboss.

5   To change the colour of the text, click on the arrow to the right of the Color list and click on the desired colour.

6   Click on `OK` to apply the new look to your text.

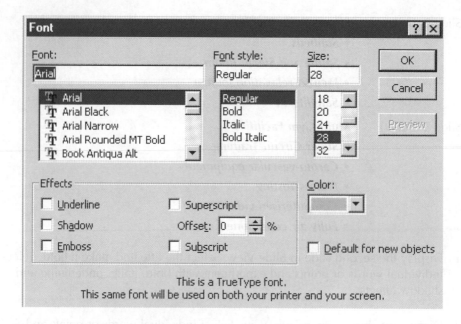

Task 3: Further formatting

1 Open the presentation **Facility** in Slide View.

2 Display the title slide. Select the title and try changing the font, and checking Emboss in the Font dialog box.

3 Display the second slide. After **Sauna and Steam Room** add the text (*35°C*) select the o and use Format-Font and check the Superscript box. Click on **OK** and this should now read (35°C).

4 Save the presentation.

Formatting paragraphs – alignment and line spacing

Alignment is the way in which text appears between the left and right margins. In PowerPoint there are four types of alignment:

1 left alignment – aligns text along the left margin.

2 right alignment – aligns text along the right margin.

3 centre alignment – aligns text in the centre of the slide/page.

4 justified text – text is aligned with both left and right margins.

The amount of space between lines in a paragraph and the space between paragraphs can be controlled using the Line Spacing dialog box. This can be summoned by choosing Format-Line Spacing. The box contains three fields:

Line Spacing   The number of units of space between lines in the paragraph.

Before Paragraph   The number of units of space before the first line in the paragraph.

After Paragraph   The number of units of space after the last line in the paragraph.

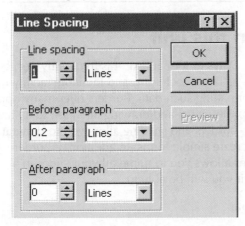

Select the number of units you require using the **Increase** or **Decrease** buttons or by keying in a number directly. You can see the effect of these changes on the slide as you make them by clicking on the **Preview** button. If the dialog box obscures the slide then move it by dragging its title bar.

Task 4: Line spacing

1 Open the presentation **Facility** and add a new slide after the second slide. Choose a bullet layout for the slide. Leave the title blank and add the following quote after the bullet point.

    I felt so much more relaxed and ready to cope with the stress of everyday living after I used the Fitness Suite facilities

2 Select the text and choose Format-Line Spacing. Alter the line spacing to 1.5 and click on the **Preview** button to see the effect of the change. You may have to move the dialog box out of the way to see it. Click on **OK**

3 Add another bullet slide at the end of the presentation. Enter the following text in the bullet point.

    The Multi-Gym facilities have enabled me to enhance my fitness level so that I have more stamina to win.

4 Choose Format-Line Spacing. Alter the spacing before to 0.5 and make the line spacing 2. Click on the **Preview** button to see the effect of the change. Click on **OK** .

5 Save and view the presentation before closing it.

Using tables and borders

What you will learn in this unit

Tables and borders offer two different ways to format text. It is frequently necessary to be able to present text or numbers as lists in columns, and the table facility offers a flexible means of presenting and formatting such data. Borders offer many opportunities for making slides look more professional and drawing attention to a chart or a specific item of text. Used together, borders and shading allow you to draw attention to specific cells in a table or to create simple forms. In addition, a border around the total text on a Slide Master allows you to frame all your slides in a consistent way. By the end of this unit you will be able to:

- use the table feature to create a table
- format text in a table
- apply borders and shading to text
- apply borders and shading to text in tables.

Using the table feature to create a table

This activity accesses the Microsoft Word table feature from within PowerPoint.

1   Open a presentation and choose a slide on to which you wish to enter the table, then click on Insert-Microsoft Word Table.

2   Insert a new slide using the   New Slide   button and then choose a Table Slide Layout and double-click on Table Placeholder.

3   The Insert Word Table dialog box appears. Choose the number of columns and click on   OK .

4   The Tables and Borders toolbar appears. Use the tools and menus to create the table.

5   When the table is created click anywhere on the slide to return to PowerPoint.

The table is inserted in the current slide. It can be moved, sized, coloured, and shadows and frames may be added.

Task 1: Creating a table

1   Open the presentation **Project.**

2   Insert a new slide after the existing slide that is headed **Preferred Configuration** by clicking on the   New Slide   button. This will display the New Slide dialog box. Choose a Table Slide Layout.

3 Double-click on the Table Placeholder. In the dialog box, select 2 columns and 8 rows.

4 Enter the following text in the columns. Do not worry about formatting the table (for example, right aligning the figures) as this is considered below.

Pec Deck	*2,070*
Chest Press	*2.070*
Lat. Pulldown	*1,860*
Shoulder Press	*1,990*
Thigh extension	*1,950*
Thigh curl	*1,850*
Total hip	*1,990*
Total	*15,305*

5 Use the **Autosum** button on the Tables and Borders toolbar to sum the column and calculate the total figure.

   Click off the table area to view the text in the table displayed as a slide. Quite possibly the text will not fit within the boundaries of the slide, or alternatively it may not be sufficiently large to accommodate the whole slide. The next activity deals with formatting text in tables.

Editing and formatting text in a table

Once you have created a table on a PowerPoint slide, it may be edited or formatted. To re-activate the table so that it may be edited or formatted:

■ double click on the table. If necessary, use the **Zoom** field on the Standard toolbar to increase the size of the presentation.

You may then proceed to edit, select or format text in the same way as you would for a Word table. Here we comment specifically on some of the types of formatting that are possible and in the task you will apply some of this formatting.

To format text in a table it is first necessary to select it. It is possible to select characters, words, cells or columns and rows and to format each in turn.

Some useful facilities are:

1 changing column widths by dragging column boundaries

2 changing row heights by dragging the markers around the edge of the table

3 formatting the font by using Format-Font; this summons the Font dialog box which allows you to choose the font, the font style and the font size

4 aligning data so that it aligns appropriately within columns, using the **Alignment** buttons on the toolbar.

Options on the Tables and Borders toolbar include: line style, line weight, border colour, border, shading colour, merge cells, split cells, alignment of text in cells, change text direction, sort and Table AutoFormat. You can experiment with the table AutoFormats. We have not explored these further here.

Task 2: Table formatting

We wish to improve on the formatting of the table slide that we created in the last task. Display the slide on the screen.

1 Double click on the table to activate the table for editing.

2 Select the second column and apply right justification by clicking on the
   Right Align button. This causes the numbers to be aligned appropriately.

3 Select the whole table and undertake some formatting to the font.

   ■ Choose Format-Font. Select an appropriate font, choose the font style Bold
   Italic and a font size of 28.

4 You may now find it useful to move the column boundary so that each of the
   text entries in the first column fits on one line. Subsequent to this you may need
   to move the row boundaries up.

5 Exit from the Table function by clicking on the slide outside the table.

6 Check that the text now fits on the slide; you may reposition it by dragging. If it
   still does not fit, perform some additional formatting of the type that you have
   just performed and try again!

Applying borders and shading to text

The appearance of slides can be improved significantly if borders and shading are applied appropriately. Borders and shading can be put around any object including text, graphs and images. PowerPoint automatically adds a thin line to any object that you draw. Borders can be deleted, their styles changed, colours added and weights changed.

To add a border, first select the object to which you wish to add the border by clicking on it, then choose Format-Colors and Lines. This displays the Colors and Lines dialog box, as shown below.

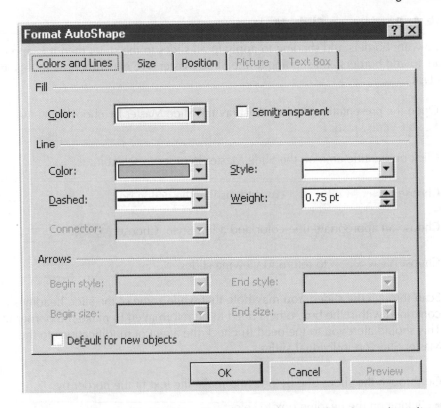

The options on this dialog box allow you to set the Fill and its colour, line colour, line styles, dashed lines and arrowheads on lines.

Once you have selected an appropriate combination choose **OK** to apply the borders.

Task 3: Borders

This task experiments with applying borders to text and tables on slides.

1   In the presentation **Project** display the slide entitled **Chelmer Leisure Centre**. Click on the body of the text to select it. Choose Format-Colors and Lines. Choose an appropriate line style. Click on **OK**. Examine the effect of the border.

2   Move to the slide entitled: **Atlanta Sports Proposal**. This slide has a table embedded in it. Click on the table so the handles appear to show that it is selected. Choose Format-Colors and Lines. In the Colors and Lines. dialog box, choose an appropriate line style. Click on **OK**. Examine the effect of the border. Save the presentation.

   To remove or change a border, display the Colors and Lines. box and change the selection. To remove a border, choose None.

Task 4: Borders on Slide Master

If you want borders and shading to apply to all slides in the suite, then it is appropriate to add borders and shading to the Slide Master. We experiment with this in this task.

1   Open the presentation **Project**. Display the Slide Master by choosing View-Master-Slide Master.

2   Click on the title area on the Slide Master in order to select it.

3   Choose Format-Colors and Lines to display the dialog box.

4   Choose an appropriate line color and a line style. Choose **OK** .

5   Choose View-Slides to return to viewing slides.

6   Scan through the slides. You may note that while some of the slide headings are contained within the box, others need to be reformatted to make the border fit. This should alert you to the need to check the affect of modifications to the Master Slide on individual slides.

7   Go through the slides one by one and make the text fit the border by:
   ■ clicking on the heading box to select it
   ■ making the text a little smaller using Format-Font, and choosing a font size
   ■ dragging the borders of the box to accommodate the text
   ■ checking that the text and the box are still on the slide
   ■ on the title slide, either selecting and deleting the box altogether, or expanding it considerably so that it accommodates the title text.

8   Save and view the presentation.

Applying borders and shading to text in tables

Task 3 applied a border around the edge of a table. It is also possible to apply borders and shading more selectively to text in tables, so that specific cells can be highlighted or, in a more elaborate way, forms can be created for screen display. Essentially different borders or shading can be applied to any part of a table. We illustrate this through two examples.

You may find that, although you can create and format the table, when you try to insert the table into a PowerPoint slide not all the borders and shading are displayed. This is a feature of PowerPoint 97 and not an error on your part.

Task 5 Shading in a table

In the presentation **Project** display the slide entitled: **Atlanta Sports Proposal**.

1   Double click on the table to display it as a table. Click on the bottom row of the table and choose Table-Select Row to select it.

2   Choose Format-Borders and Shading. This will open the Borders and Shading dialog box.

3   Click on the **Borders** tab, then choose Grid and a line style. In the Apply to box select Cell.

4   Click on the **Shading** tab to display the Shading dialog box. Choose 10% in the Style field and Cell in the Apply to field. Choose **OK** .

5   Click outside the table to return to the slide. The bottom row of the table should now display a border and shading.

   If the text disappears it has faded into the shading, so try an alternative shading.

Task 6 Table borders and shading

If you have worked through the companion volume on Word 97 basic skills you will already have created this table. Visit Unit 14 to learn how to import the table into PowerPoint.

In this task we will create a new presentation with just one slide, which the manager can use in his weekly staff briefing and then reproduce as a paper schedule for distribution. The slide contains a table showing the scheduling of classes as shown below.

1   Open a new blank presentation and choose a table slide. Enter the heading, *Activity Timetable* and format and centre the text.

2   Double-click on the Table Placeholder. Create a blank table with six columns and eight rows.

3   Enter the text given below into the table.

4   Select the table, and apply borders using Format-Borders and Shading. You may find that borders do not appear as you want them in PowerPoint. There is little you can do about this. Apply a Grid.

5   Select appropriate cells and apply shading using Format-Borders and Shading.

6   Adjust the formatting of the text and vary the column width to make the text fit the table.

7   Save the presentation as **Timetable**.

FITNESS SUITE	Monday	Tuesday	Wednesday	Thursday	Friday
Daytime					
10.00 - 11.00am	Ladies' Aerobics	Men's Multi-gym	Ladies Aerobics		Body Conditioning
11.00 - 12.00pm	Weight Training			Weight Training	Step Aerobics
2.00 - 3.00pm		Ladies' Multi-gym	Body Conditioning	Step Aerobics	Men's Multi-gym
3.00 - 4.00pm	Body conditioning		Weight Training	Multi-gym	
Evening					
7.00 - 9.00pm	Step Aerobics	Family Multi-gym	Weight Training	Body Conditioning	

Using text boxes

What you will learn in this unit

When you create slides using Slide Layout, PowerPoint provides sections on the slide for adding text. Generally these are titles and bullet points and text can be added by pointing, clicking and keying in. The areas in which this text is held are known as text placeholders. If you wish to add text that you do not want in a standard placeholder then the **Text Box** button on the Drawing toolbar can be used to add this text.

Standard text placeholders tend to have pre-set bullet formatting. You may wish to add a piece of descriptive text where you want the left and indent margins both set to 0cm. Remind yourself of some of the odd effects when creating the slides in the presentation **Advert**. You may wish to position text in different parts of a slide as illustrated at the end of Task 3 below. You may wish to set your own formatting in terms of margin and tab position, for example, to line up lists of text and figures. Using text boxes or a combination of text boxes, therefore, provides you with a comprehensive range of word processing features.

By the end of this unit you will be able to:

- add text to a slide which is outside a placeholder
- edit and format this text
- move the text on the slide.

Creating Text Boxes

To add text other than a slide title or main text, text boxes can be used. This Text Box tool ▣ can be used in either of two ways:

- click on the **Text Box** tool in the Drawing toolbar and click on the slide and begin typing straight away

or

- click on the **Text Box** tool and click and drag a text box on the slide, then key in your text to this box.

If you don't drag a text box first then the line of text will just get longer as you type since the word-wrap facility is off, so unless you are adding only a small amount of text then it is better to drag a text box first.

 A text box added using the first method may later be resized and the text enclosed will wrap within the resized box.

If a text box doesn't give the desired effect then it may be deleted, but remember that the text it encloses will also be deleted, so you may wish to copy it to the clipboard first.

Task 1: Creating a text box

In this task adding the two types of text box will be considered. A text box is to be used to add the name of the course and institution of the student creating the presentation **Project**. Before you begin, make sure that the Drawing toolbar is displayed.

1 Open the presentation **Project** and display the title slide in Slide View.

2 Click on the text box buttons and click at the left side of the slide below the name of the student.

3 Begin typing straight away and key in *HND Business and Finance Manchester Metropolitan University*. Note that the text box grows to the right as this text is keyed in. Note that when you are keying text into a text box the edges of the box are shown by (non-printing) closely spaced short diagonal lines.

4 When you have finished keying in the text click anywhere else on the slide.

To investigate the drag method of text box creation we will remove this text box, but before doing this we will copy the text to the clipboard so that it can be pasted into the new text box.

5 Click at the beginning of the text in the text box and drag so that it is highlighted. Next use Edit-Copy to copy this to the clipboard.

6 Next click on the border of the text box to select the text box. Delete the box by pressing the *Delete* key.

7 Click on the text box button. This time click the cursor on the slide, starting slightly to the left and below the student's name and dragging to the right and slightly downwards. When you release the mouse button a text box of the width you drew is shown and, as the word wrap facility is on, as text is keyed in the box it will grow downwards instead of to the right as previously.

8 The insertion point is at the top left of the box ready for text to be keyed in. Paste in the text from the clipboard using Edit-Paste. Save the presentation. If your box is not quite the right size don't worry, as this is considered below.

Sizing and moving text boxes

Before a text box can be sized or moved it must be selected. To select a text box click anywhere on its border (to display the border click on any of the text within the text box). The border changes to a shaded line composed of dots and at the corners and in the middle of each side are rectangles known as sizing handles. Generally, dragging one of the sizing handles will alter the shape of the box but this is influenced by the settings in the Text Anchor dialog box (see below). To move a text box click and drag the border (not a sizing handle).

Text anchors

Text is 'anchored' to a point in the text box, for example if text is anchored to the top of the box then dragging the box at the bottom to make it larger will not have any effect. You can use anchors to make text appear at the top, the middle, or the bottom of a text box although the effect is better appreciated when text is put inside a shape which will be considered in Unit 13. You can also set the size of the margins that surround the text.

Set an anchor point for text and/or adjust the margins surrounding text in a text box as follows.

1   Select the text box you wish to realign.

2   Choose Format-Text Box. The Format Text Box dialog box appears. Click on the 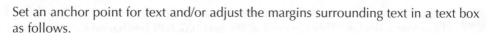 tab.

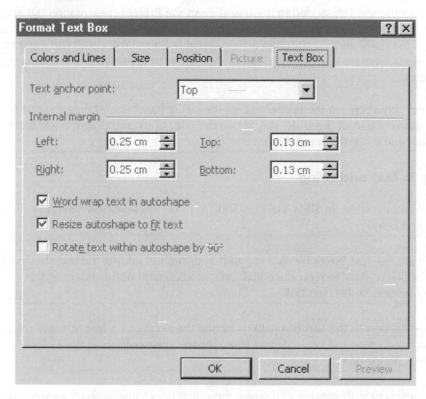

3   In the drop-down Text Anchor Point box, select the anchor point you want for your text.

4   In the Internal margin section adjust the margins either by using the up or down arrows to increase or decrease the margin or by typing in the measurement directly.

5   If the dialog box is obscuring your view then drag it to another part of the screen.

6   When you find a design that you like, choose **OK**.

There are also three other options available through the Text Box dialog box. These are Word wrap text in Autoshape, Resize autoshape to fit text and Rotate text within autoshape by 90°. If the first two of these are both checked then the word-wrap facility is on and the box adjusts to fit the text, which is why dragging a sizing handle may not have any effect.

In the Format Text Box dialog box the option Resize Autoshape to fit text will be chosen as a default. This means that the text box will be shaped to fit the text. If this does not happen, and the text lies outside the box, click this box to rectify the situation.

Task 2: Moving and sizing text boxes

1   Select the text box added to the title slide in the **Project** presentation. Drag one of the vertical sides to adjust the width of the box so that the name of the course and the name of the institution are on separate lines. (You could use *Enter* to make a separate line but the point of this task is to investigate the word-wrap effect).

2   Click anywhere on the border except the sizing handles and drag the text box to a different part of the slide, say, above the title. Click and drag it back again. Save and close the presentation.

Task 3: Text anchoring

1   Add a new slide, in Slide View, as Slide 5, to the presentation **Advert** as illustrated below.

2   Create five text boxes by clicking and dragging and adding the text shown in the slide. Do not try to reproduce text fonts or alignment at this stage, as this will considered in the next task.

3   Add borders to the text boxes by selecting the border of a text box and using Format-Colors and Lines. Select Line, Fill and their colours in the Colors and Lines dialog box.

4   Experiment with moving and sizing these text boxes and with choosing different text anchoring options.

5   Save and close this presentation.

> **Sauna and Steam Room**
> wonderful after a hard workout, long
> day, or simply for pure relaxation

Health Suite

Our superb health suite
lets you relax and
unwind

> **Jacuzzi**
> **relaxation**
> **lounge with**
> **satellite TV**
> alleviate stress
> and unwind by
> immersing
> yourself in jets
> of warm water
> and gently
> soothing
> bubbles

> **Power Shower** whether
> you like your showers hot or
> cold, foam, spray or jet, we
> have just the shower to suit
> your needs.

> **Sunbeds** our three new
> Ultrabronze tanning beds use
> the latest RUVA tubes

Text editing and formatting

This is a very short section as text editing and formatting have been considered in other units. Text within the box may be edited, selected, deleted, dragged and dropped as in a word processor. All the activities discussed in Unit 7 can be applied to text in a text box.

Although it is generally better to use the standard slide types for bullet points, it is possible to put bullet points into a text box. Indented paragraphs may also be used within a text box. It is generally advisable to keep the same style of paragraphs within a text box as some formatting such as the indent margin applies globally within a text box. Other formatting such as paragraph alignment may be applied to individual paragraphs within the same text box.

Task 4: Text operations

Review Unit 7 before undertaking this task.

1   Spelling check the presentation **Project**.

2   Use Edit-Find to find the word 'Finance'.

3   Experiment with applying different fonts and sizes to the text in the text box.

4 Apply centre alignment and adjust the size of the box so that the title of the course and the name of the institution are on separate lines.

5 Using the Slide Master, centre the slide title text so that all titles will be centred. Save and close the presentation.

Task 5: Margins and tabs

In this task the formatting and alignment of the existing slides in the presentation **Advert** will be edited to correct their 'untidiness'.

1 In Slide View, display Slide 2 of **Advert**. Check that the ruler is on by choosing View-Ruler. In the slide, click in the main text to select it.

2 Drag the left margin (the lower triangle on the ruler) to the right, to approximately the 4cm position. This formats all except the last paragraph correctly. To apply different formatting to this last paragraph you will need to place it in a separate text box.

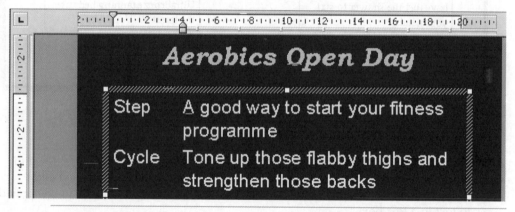

3 Select the last paragraph and use Edit-Cut to remove it and place it on the Clipboard.

4 Make the text box shorter to fit the remaining text.

5 Drag a new text box below the existing one and use Edit-Paste to add the text from the clipboard. If necessary, adjust the size and position of this box. Note that the left margin is at 0cm in this box.

6 Display Slide 3 and select its main text. Choose Insert-Tab and click on the ruler at about 10cm to place a tab. If the columns were separated by a tab character (if not, then replace any spaces with a tab character), then the second column should move to the new position.

7   Move on to Slide 4 and select its main text. Set the left margin to 0cm by using the two triangles on the ruler. In the price list check that there is one tab character between the columns (delete any extra ones).

8   Set a left tab on the ruler at 4cm. Select a right tab by clicking on the tab type selector to the left of the ruler until it displays a backwards L (see illustration below).

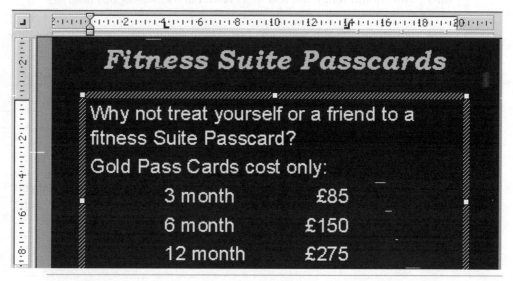

9   Click on the ruler at 14cm to place a right tab. The price list should line up on its right hand edge. Save the presentation.

10 Repeat the task for Slide 3 of the presentation **Advert1**, setting the left tab at 1cm and the right tab at 19cm.

11 Save the presentation.

 Tabs may be removed from the ruler by dragging them off it, downwards.

Task 6: Paragraph formatting within text boxes

In this task, some paragraph formatting will be explored using the text box slide in **Advert**. This should be taken as a starting point for paragraph formatting and the Help facility may be consulted for more information.

1   Display the text box slide (Slide 5) in **Advert** in Slide View.

2   Click in the text of the 'Power Shower' box and choose View-Ruler. This displays a ruler for this text box.

3   Click on the **Bullets** button in the toolbar and a bullet point appears at the beginning of the paragraph. Next drag the left margin (the lower triangle on the ruler) to the right a little way; this will create a hanging indent for the bullet.

4   Now remove the bullet by clicking again on the **Bullets** button and then drag the left margin back to line up with the indent margin (upper triangle on the ruler). This should return the text to its layout at the start of this task.

5   Now click in the 'Health Suite' text box. There should be a new line separating 'Health Suite' from the following text. If there isn't, add one.

6   Apply different paragraph alignment to these two paragraphs using the alignment buttons in the toolbar. Finish by applying centre alignment to both.

7   Save the presentation.

8   In the 'Power Shower' text box illustrated there is a full stop (period) at the end of the paragraph. In slides with bullet points you may find that you have been inconsistent with the use of full stops. You can check for inconsistencies using Tools-Style checker, ticking the Case and end punctuation check box and choosing Options to select the type of punctuation you want.

Using clip art and WordArt

What you will learn in this unit

PowerPoint offers a large choice of professionally produced clip art that you can add to your slides. If the choice of clip art is not appropriate then if you have some other artwork or a scanned image these may be inserted into your presentation. WordArt can be used to attract the eye to a slide, particularly an auto running presentation, which may be being used for advertising. Additional enhancements include movies (videos) and sound.

By the end of this unit you should be able to:

- select and insert clip art in a slide

- create and position WordArt on a slide

- insert pictures

- appreciate the mechanisms for adding sound and/or video to your presentation.

Inserting clip art

PowerPoint comes with many clip art images and to make selection of these easy there is the ClipArt Gallery. The ClipArt Gallery allows you to choose from different categories of clip art and will display the selection available in that category. Insert a clip art image into a slide as follows.

1   Working in Slide View, select the slide to which the clip art is to be added.

2   Choose Insert-Picture-Clip Art or click on the   Insert ClipArt   button. Alternatively, if a Clip Art and Text Layout is chosen from the New Slide dialog box, double-click on the Clip Art placeholder. The Microsoft ClipArt Gallery dialog box appears. In this dialog box you will see a preview selection of clip art images. Note that you may have to wait a little while (depending on the number of categories you have installed) for the gallery to open for the first time.

3   From the list of categories, select the category from which to choose an image.

4   Choose an image by scrolling through those presented and click on the one most appropriate to your slide.

5   Clicking on   Insert   will place the image on the slide. The image is placed in a clip art placeholder, which allows the image to be moved and resized.

 AutoClipArt can help you match your ideas to relevant clip art. Choose Tools-AutoClipArt.

Task 1: Adding clip art

1   Open the presentation **Briefing** in Slide View. Add another slide at the end of this presentation, choosing a Clip Art and Text Layout. Add the title *New Branch Opens.*

2   Delete the text placeholder and re-size the ClipArt placeholder to fit the slide. For a wider range of clip art insert your Office 97 CD-ROM into your CD-ROM drive. Double-click on the ClipArt placeholder, choose the category Buildings and select a piece of clip art that looks like an office. Click on ▮ **Insert** ▮.

3   Save the presentation.

Moving the image on the slide

Images are held in a placeholder. When the image is selected the placeholder handles can be seen. These are eight small rectangles at the corners and halfway along the edges of a rectangle bounding the image.

Move a clip art object as follows.

1   Select the clip art object by clicking on it.

2   Use the arrow keys to move the object up, down, to the left or to the right, or click anywhere on the image except the handles and drag.

Re-size an image as follows.

1   Select the clip art object.

2   Click and drag one of the sizing handles. Note that dragging a corner handle will keep the proportions of the image constant.

To delete an image, select it and press *Delete*.

Several images may be placed on the same slide and by arranging them on your slide a composite image may be built up. Images can be layered and the order of layering can be changed to achieve the desired result. A slide may be positioned thus, using the Draw drop down list at the bottom of the screen.

Command	Effect
Draw-Order-Bring to Front	Brings an image to the top of the layers
Draw-Order-Send to Back	Sends an image to the bottom of the layers
Draw-Order-Bring Forward	Moves an image up one layer
Draw-Order-Send Backward	Moves an image down one layer

Picture Toolbar

Pictures, or clip art can be formatted through the use of the buttons on the Picture toolbar. These include buttons to:

- insert a picture
- change a colour image to greyscale
- adjust the contrast of the picture using the two contrast buttons
- adjust the brightness of the picture using the two brightness buttons
- crop (i.e. cut to size) a picture
- choose a line style for the image border
- control text wrapping
- display the format picture dialog box
- set a transparent colour and
- reset the picture.

These controls will be explored in the following task.

Task 2: Picture formatting

1 Add another slide to the presentation **Briefing**. Choose a Text and Clip Art Layout. Add the title *Computer training*. Add the bullet points:

- *1st October 1999*
- *Trainer's visits*
- *Contact IT Support*

2 For a wider range of clip art insert your Office 97 CD-ROM into your CD-ROM drive. Double-click on the Clip Art placeholder, choose the category Academic and select a piece of clip art that gives the impression of computer training. Click on **Insert** .

3 Add a ClipArt and Text Layout slide and the title *Investors in people*, and add the first clip art from the People at Work category. Add the bullet point:

- *Contact John Wall, Deputy Personnel Manager*

4 Save the presentation.

5   Select the clip art picture just inserted and experiment with the following using the Picture toolbar accessed via View-Toolbars-Picture.

■ Click on the **Image Control** button and investigate the effect of Greyscale and Black and White. You can return the image to normal using the Automatic setting.

■ Increase and reduce the contrast and the brightness of the image.

■ Add a border using the **Line Color** and **Line Style** buttons. This can be removed by choosing More Lines and selecting No Line.

■ Try cropping the picture using the Crop tool, for example, to select out the head and shoulders of the centre figure.

■ Finally, to put the picture back to its original form try the **Reset Picture** button but be prepared for the image to return to the size it was when first inserted.

6   Close the presentation.

Task 3: Arranging clip art on a slide

In this task a blank slide will be created and three images added to it. The effect of sizing, moving, layering and colouring these images will be explored. This task is most effective with images from the Sports and Leisure category; if this is not available try to find three images from a category that is available to you.

1   Add a blank slide to the end of the presentation **Advert**.

2   Click on the **Clip Art** button on the Standard toolbar and select the Sports category. Scroll down through the images available on the CD to find images of leisure centre type sports.

3   Select a suitable image and click on **Insert** · The image will be placed in a placeholder on the slide.

4   Using the sizing handles investigate re-sizing the image. Experiment with moving the image on the slide.

5   Add a second image by clicking on the **Clip Art** button. Choose another image from the Sports category.

6   Size and position this image. Add a third image and size and position this. Select one of the images and click on the **Recolor Picture** button on the Picture toolbar and change the colours in this image, trying to blend them with your slide colour scheme.

7   Move the images so that they overlap and experiment with the effect of selecting an image and using   **Send to Back** ,   **Bring to Front** ,   **Send Backwards** , and   **Bring Forwards** . Save the presentation.

Adding WordArt

WordArt allows text to be stylised by presenting it in different shapes, for example text may be slanted or curved. Add WordArt as follows.

1   Select, in Slide View, the slide to which the WordArt is to be added.

2   Click on the   **Insert-WordArt**   button on the Drawing toolbar. (To display the Drawing toolbar, click on View-Toolbars-Drawing).

3   Select a WordArt style from the WordArt Gallery. Click on   **OK** .

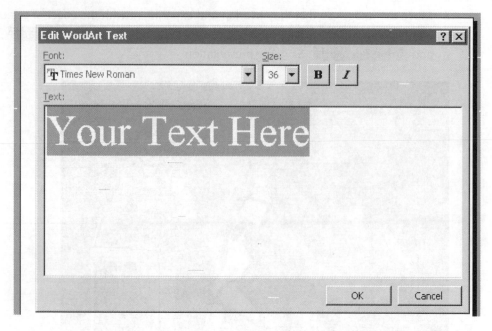

4   Enter the text for your WordArt into the Edit WordArt Text dialog box. Click on
    OK .

5   To delete a WordArt object simply select it and press *Delete*.

Task 4: Adding WordArt

This task explores some of the WordArt features described above.

1   Add another blank slide, in Slide View, to the end of the presentation **Advert**.

2   Click on the **Insert-WordArt** button on the **Drawing** toolbar.

3   Choose a WordArt style from the WordArt Gallery. Click on **OK** .

4   Add the text *Chelmer Leisure* and click on **OK** .

5   Click on the slide and experiment with moving and sizing the WordArt object on
    the slide.

6   Add another WordArt object with the text *Fitness Suite*. Experiment with layering
    the two WordArt objects. Now select and delete the second WordArt object by
    pressing *Delete*.

7   Click on the **Edit Text** button on the WordArt toolbar to edit the first WordArt
    object to read

> **Chelmer Leisure and**
> **Fitness Suite**
> **Recreation Centre**

and choose a suitable font.

8   Click on the   WordArt shape   button in the WordArt toolbar and
    select the shape (fourth one, second row). You can change the colour of
    the text using the   Format WordArt   button and selecting Fill-Effects from
    the drop down menu. Save the presentation. Look at the presentation in Slide
    Sorter View and move this slide to the beginning of the presentation. Save the
    presentation.

Task 5: Using the WordArt toolbar

Once you have created a piece of WordArt, the tools on the WordArt toolbar can be
used to create a range of different effects. The table below shows some of the effects
that can be created by clicking on the different buttons on the toolbar. Take a piece
of WordArt that you have created and try to replicate the effects in this table. Note
that we have not made use of colour since this book is printed in black and white,
but you may also like to experiment with the use of colours and choose colours in
keeping with the slide's colour scheme.

Button	Function	Example
	Format WordArt	 Chelmer
	Choose a WordArt shape	 Chelmer Leisure
	Rotate WordArt	 Chelmer Leisure

Adjust WordArt letter heights

 Swop from horizontal to vertical text and (vice versa)

 Adjust alignment

 Adjust letter spacing

Inserting scanned pictures

If you need a specific image for your presentation you may be able to acquire it by scanning a photograph or drawing or by creating it using another application. If you have a scanner attached to your computer and want to scan in images directly then you will need to check that you have installed Microsoft Photo Editor from the Office CD. You will find this application in the Office Tools group. To scan and insert a picture into a slide

1   Working in Slide View, select the slide to which the picture is to be added.

2   Choose Insert-Picture-From Scanner and Microsoft Photo Editor starts which in turn starts your scanner software. Scan the image using your scanner. The image appears in the Photo Editor window where you can manipulate it before using File-Exit and Return to Presentation to embed the image in the slide.

Inserting picture files

You may have an image file that you want to add to a slide.

1   Choose Insert-Picture-From File and the Insert Picture dialog box appears. This dialog box is similar to the Open dialog box and you can specify the drive and directory in which the picture file can be found. In the Files of Type list box you may select the format of your picture. Graphics files take many different formats and PowerPoint can import a wide range of picture formats.

2   Select the name of the picture file and click on **Insert**.

3   The picture is placed in a placeholder, allowing the image to be moved and resized.

4   Pictures can be deleted as for other objects.

Task 6: Adding a picture

In this task, a scanned image of the Fitness Suite layout will be added to the presentation **Project**. The layout is shown below so that you can scan it to try out this task.

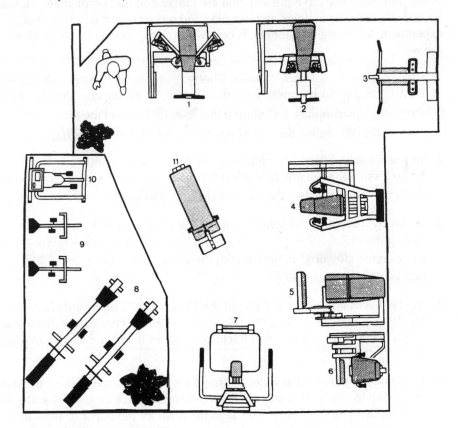

1   Scan the layout and save it as **Layout** or try scanning the picture directly. Open the presentation **Project**.

2 In Slide View add a new slide after the table slide following the **Atlanta Sports Proposal** slide.

3 From the New Slide dialog box select a title only layout. Edit the title to read *Atlanta Suite Plan*.

4 Either choose Insert-Picture-From File or Insert-Picture-From Scanner. If you are scanning then use your scanner software as usual and then embed the image from Photo Editor. If you are inserting the file **Layout** then, from the Insert Picture dialog box select the picture file **Layout** and click on **Insert** .

5 The picture is placed in the placeholder, and it can be moved and resized to suit the slide. Try moving the title upwards and expanding the picture by dragging one corner to fill the slide. Save the presentation.

Sound and video

There will be no task associated with this activity. However, the basics of adding sound and video clips to a presentation are introduced for completeness. If you have multimedia capabilities and can play and record sound or video digitally then experiment, following the guidelines below. A sound clip may be inserted as follows.

1 Choose Insert-Movies and Sounds. Choose Sound from Gallery. Alternatively, if the ClipArt Layout is chosen from the AutoLayout dialog box, double-click on the ClipArt placeholder and choose the **Sounds** tab on the Microsoft ClipArt Gallery list box. Select the sound you want and click on **Insert** .

2 To insert a sound from file, choose Insert-Movies and Sounds – Sound from File. In the Insert Sound dialog box select the drive and directory (folder) where the file is to be found, select the file and click on **Insert** .

3 To directly record sound (usually speech via a microphone), choose Insert-Movies and Sounds – Record Sound. The Sound Recorder dialog box appears. Click on the **Record** button, record the sound and click on the **Stop** button, then click on **OK** .

4 To play tracks from a music CD, put the CD in the CD drive and choose Insert-Movies and Sounds – Play CD audio track. A dialog box appears that allows you to select the start track and end track. You can set the sound to play in a looped mode.

5 Sound files are inserted as objects. They look like small speakers on the slide and are played by double-clicking on them. Music CD track objects look like a CD but note that you must have the CD in the drive for the music to play. By adjusting play settings you can play a music CD track or tracks throughout your presentation.

The play settings for the embedded sound may be adjusted as follows.

1   Select the sound object and choose Slide Show-Custom Animation.

2   Under the Play Settings tab of the dialog box tick the Play using animation order check box. You can select the settings you require, for example determining the number of slides for which the sound will play. The Hide while not playing check box will control whether or not the icon is displayed on the slide when the slide show is run.

3   The timing of the playing of the sound can be set using the Timing tab of the dialog box. The choices are:

   ■ play when sound object is clicked

   ■ play automatically a specified number of seconds after the last event.

4   Click on OK . Run the presentation.

The procedure to add a video clip or movie is very similar. There are some movies available from the movie gallery on the Office CD that you could try embedding into a slide.

Colour schemes and backgrounds

What you will learn in this unit

Colour schemes are sets of eight professionally balanced colours designed to be used as the main colours of a slide presentation. A colour scheme makes it easy to create professional looking slides and to change the colours on the slides of the presentation. If you change your colour scheme PowerPoint can update your slides for you. Each colour scheme controls the colour of the background, lines, text, shadows, fills and other items on a slide. Until now we have used the default colour scheme available when you open a blank presentation. At the end of this unit you will be able to:

- understand the terminology associated with colour schemes

- select a colour scheme

- create and change colour schemes

- change the background design.

 This unit is not applicable if you are seeking to create black and white transparency slides.

Understanding colour schemes and backgrounds

Before seeking to apply colours it is useful to explain some of the terms associated with colour schemes. You will see some of these terms used on the Slide Colour Scheme dialog box displayed below.

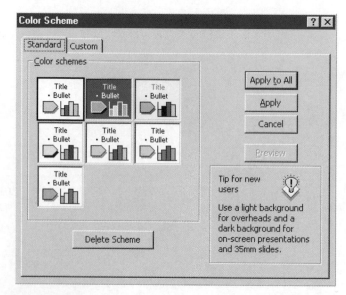

Colour schemes A colour scheme is the basic set of eight colours that you apply to a slide, to notes pages and to audience handouts. A colour scheme consists of a background colour, a colour for lines and text and six remaining colours. Every colour menu lists the colour scheme colours as your options. You can further customise your choices by adding colours to drop down menus such as Fill Colour, Shadow Colour and Line Colour.

Other colours are non scheme colours that you use for a special purpose, such as flags and clip art. Non-scheme colours are not changed when you change your colour scheme.

Background colour is the underlying colour.

Text and lines colour is used for writing text and drawing lines on the slide.

Shadows colour is used for shadows. It is often a darker shade of a background colour.

Title text colour is used for the title text.

Fills colour is one that contrasts with both the background and the lines and text colours. The fills colour is used on graphs.

Accent colours are designed to work as colours for secondary features on a slide. Accent colours are also used as colours on graphs. There are also accent colours for hyperlinks and followed hyperlinks.

 The colours that you see depend upon the video card in your computer.

Selecting and creating a colour scheme

Colour schemes can be applied to one slide or all the slides in a presentation. Normally it is best to work on the colour scheme for the presentation first.

You may select an existing colour scheme as follows.

1   With a presentation displayed and one slide selected, choose Format-Slide Color Scheme. The Color Scheme dialog box appears.

2   Click on one of the displayed colour schemes and click on **Apply** (to apply only to the displayed slide) or **Apply to All** .

You may create a new colour scheme as follows.

1   With a presentation displayed and one slide selected, choose Format-Slide Color Scheme. The Color Scheme dialog box appears.

2   Click on the **Custom** tab.

3   Click on the Background Colour and choose **Change Color** . Select the colour you want to use for the slide background. When you select the background colour, the text colours change to co-ordinate with the background colour.

79

4   Choose a Text & Lines colour.

5   Choose any other colours that you wish to change.

6   Click on the **Apply** button to apply the new colour scheme only to this slide, or click on **Apply to All** to apply the colour scheme to all the slides in the presentation.

7   If you like your new scheme, return to the Color Scheme dialog box and in the Custom sub-dialog box, click on **Add as Standard Sheme**. This will add your new scheme to the set of standard schemes.

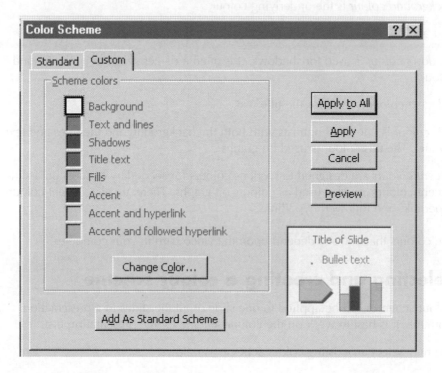

Task 1: Colour schemes

Open the presentation **Advert.** Experiment with applying different colour schemes to the presentation. If you are working in a group discuss your preferred colour scheme with someone else. Ask them what message the colour scheme communicates.

Choose a colour scheme that would be suitable for:

■ a formal presentation of a consultancy report

■ an autorunning presentation to be displayed on an exhibition stand

■ a student project presentation in an assessment situation.

Explain why you think that your chosen colour schemes are suitable for these purposes.

Creating a new colour in a colour scheme

Individual colours can be changed in the colour scheme, for example, to match a company colour or match the colour of the company's logo.

You may change a colour in the colour scheme as follows.

1   Display or select the slide whose colour scheme you want to change.

2   Choose Format-Slide Color Scheme, and the Color Scheme dialog box appears. Click on the ` Custom ` tab.

3   Click on a colour that you want to change (note the labels).

4   Click on the ` Change Color ` button. The Color dialog box for the selected colour appears.

5   Click on the colour that you want to use. If you want to create your own colour, you can click on the ` Custom ` button, and adjust the Hue, Saturation and Luminance to create the desired colour.

6   Click on ` OK ` which will return you to the Color Scheme dialog box.

7   Repeat the above steps to change any other colours.

8   When you have finished changing colours, click on the ` Apply ` or ` Apply to All ` button. (See the Color Scheme dialog box at beginning of this unit.)

Task 2: Logo

Choose a logo of an organisation with which you are associated, and on a new slide in a new presentation, try to replicate the logo in the right colour. Save the presentation as **Logo**.

Applying customised colour schemes to other presentations

Once you have created your own colour scheme, you may wish to apply it to other presentations, so that you can develop a house style for presentation colour. Alternatively, you may choose to use an organisation-wide colour scheme as a default for all presentations and to modify the scheme a little for individual presentations.

You may copy a colour scheme from one presentation to another as follows.

1   Open the presentation that has the colour scheme that you want to copy.

2   Choose View-Slide Sorter, or click on the ` Slide Sorter ` button.

3 Click on the slide that you want to copy.

4 Click on the **Format Painter** button.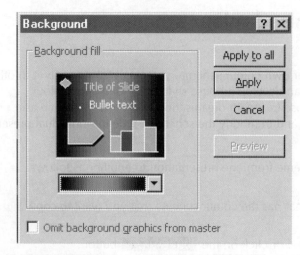

5 Open the presentation to which you wish to apply the colour scheme.

6 Choose View-Slide Sorter, or click on the **Slide Sorter** button.

7 Click on the slides to which you wish to apply the copied colour scheme.

The alternative approach is to create a new standard colour scheme as above and to apply this to the second presentation.

Task 3: Customising colour schemes

Using the slide that you created in the last task, create a second copy by opening the file and saving it under a different name, as a separate presentation. Customise the colour scheme on this copy. Now apply this new colour scheme to your first version of the slide, so that the two slides appear the same again.

Adding a background design to slides

Custom backgrounds are easy to create and can achieve a dramatic effect. You can change the background to individual slides or to the whole presentation. To change the background to the whole presentation, either work on the Slide Master, or choose the **Apply to All** button.

Change the background design as follows.

1 Display the slide whose background you want to change.

2 Choose Format-Background; the Background dialog box appears.

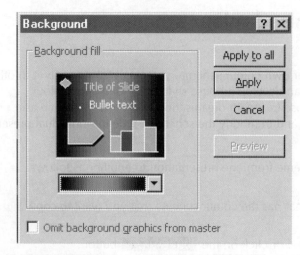

3 Select one of the options in the Background Fill colour drop down box.

4 Choose an appropriate Fill effect and click on **OK** .

5 Click on the **Apply** button to apply the background only to a selected slide, or **Apply to All** to apply the background to all the slides in this presentation.

Task 4: Background shading

Open the presentation **Logo** that you created in Task 2 above. Experiment with adding background shading to the slide.

Open the presentation **Advert** and apply a lighter background to the text box and sporting images slide.

Tips for using colour schemes

■ If none of the colour schemes is to your taste, try selecting a scheme that is close to what you want, and then changing either the background colour or the lines and text colour.

■ Try applying your new colour scheme to one slide. It is easy to change the slide back to its master colour scheme if you do not like the scheme.

■ With 35mm slides, dark backgrounds work best.

■ With overhead transparencies, light backgrounds are best.

■ If you have a colour printer, try picking a unique colour scheme for Notes Pages.

■ Shading applies only to the background of a slide, although you can shade a filled object.

Adding charts

What you will learn in this unit

Graph is a charting application that is embedded in Word and PowerPoint. Charts are invaluable for summarising numerical data and displaying it in an interesting and effective manner.

By the end of this unit you will be able to:

- add a chart to a presentation
- edit a chart
- format a chart
- choose a chart type.

Graph can be used to create charts and insert them into a presentation. These tasks take you step by step through the creation of a simple chart, and demonstrate how that chart can be inserted into a presentation. If you require more detailed assistance with the use of Graph please consult the companion books: S Coles and J Rowley, *Word 97 Basic Skills* and S Coles and J Rowley, *Word 97 Further Skills*.

Creating a Chart

The Microsoft Graph application shows a Datasheet window and an associated Chart window (see example opposite).

The Datasheet window is like a simple spreadsheet worksheet. Labels for data are entered in the first row and column on the data sheet. Do not type data in these cells. This first row and column remains visible as you scroll the sheet.

The data in the datasheet is displayed in the form an associated chart positioned on the slide. The chart has the following components, all of which it is possible to format.

The components of the Chart

chart	the entire area inside the border
data marker	a bar, shape or dot that marks a single data point or value
data series	a group of related data points
axis	a line that serves as a reference for plotting data on a chart
tick mark	a small line that intersects the axis and marks off a category
plot area	the area in which Graph plots the data
gridlines	lines that extent from the tick marks across the chart
chart text	text that describes data or items in a chart
legend	the key

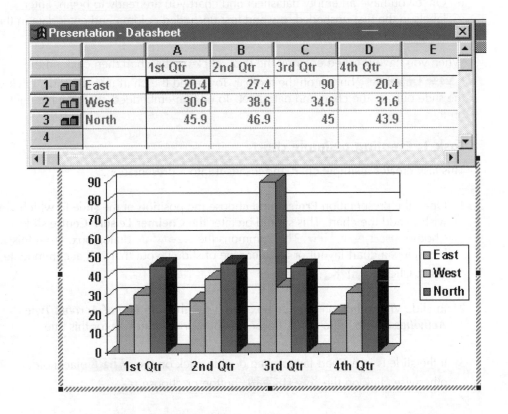

Create a basic chart as follows.

1   Choose the position of the slide to which you wish to add the chart. Choose Insert-New Slide. This summons the New Slide dialog box. From this box select a chart layout. Click on **OK**.

2   Click on the title box and insert the title into the title box.

3   Double-click on the chart placeholder. If you wish to insert a chart into a different slide layout then click on the **Insert Chart** button or choose Insert-Chart.

4   The Microsoft Graph Datasheet window and associated chart appears. It displays data that is there by default.

5   To create the graph it is necessary to enter data into the datasheet. First clear the default data from the datasheet by:

   ■ selecting the datasheet by clicking in the top left hand cell; the datasheet should be highlighted in black

   ■ choose Edit-Clear, followed by **All**, or press the *Delete* key

   ■ click on a cell in the datasheet to de-select the selection.

6   Once you have an empty datasheet and chart you are ready to begin. Enter labels in the first unshaded row and first unshaded column and enter data in the remaining cells.

When you have finished entering the data, click on the chart then click on the `View Datasheet` button on the toolbar. To embed the chart into the slide, click on the slide outside the chart and datasheet. To edit an embedded chart double-click on it.

Task 1: Creating a simple chart

This task creates a simple chart and inserts it into a presentation.

1   Open the presentation **Project** and choose the position of the slide to which you wish to add the chart. This should be after the **Chelmer Leisure Centre** slide. Choose Insert-New Slide. This summons the New Slide dialog box. From this box select a chart layout or another type of slide layout that will accommodate a chart. Click on `OK`.

2   In Slide View, click on the title box and insert the title *Use of Aerobic Type Activities* into the title box. Choose an appropriate font size for this title.

3   If the slide is in a Chart layout then double click on the `Chart` placeholder; otherwise click on the `Insert Chart` button or choose Insert-Chart.

4   The Microsoft Datasheet window appears.

5   To create the chart it is necessary to enter data into the datasheet. First clear the datasheet by:

   ■ selecting the datasheet, by clicking in the top left hand cell; the datasheet should be highlighted in black

   ■ press *Delete*

   ■ click on a cell in the datasheet to de-select the selection.

6   Once you have an empty datasheet and chart you are ready to begin. Enter labels in the first row and first column and data in the remaining cells, thus:

Aerobic Activities	Usage
Step Aerobics	5058
Popmobility	4779
Aerobics	2080
Keep Fit	679

7   When you have finished entering the data move the Datasheet window to view the Chart window. Examine the chart. You will notice that the data has been entered on the chart but that the labels and other features need formatting to improve the presentation.

8   Click on the slide to embed the chart into it.

Editing and formatting charts

In order to edit a chart it is first necessary to go back into Graph. The data on the chart can then be edited by making changes on the datasheet and the appearance of the chart can be altered by modifying the chart itself.

To edit a chart:

1   double click on the chart in your presentation

2   display the datasheet (if it does not appear) by clicking on the **View Datasheet** icon on the toolbar; make whatever changes you wish to the chart or the data.

Data on the chart can be modified by changing the data on the datasheet. It is possible to select individual cells, rows, columns and the entire datasheet. These units can then be inserted or deleted and data moved and copied.

Chart appearance can be modified by selecting different parts of the chart and applying an appropriate type of formatting.

We will not describe all the formatting operations in detail. The tasks that follow demonstrate a sufficient variety of the features to get you started. Thereafter you may like to experiment further yourself.

Task 2: Editing a chart

This task uses the datasheet to perform some simple editing on your initial chart. You may have noticed that the labels for the data appear in the legend and not on the axis. This is because the data has been treated as a set of separate data series, rather than as the items in one data series. We wish to change this.

1   Double click on the chart to enter Graph.

2   If necessary, display the datasheet by choosing View-Datasheet.

3   From the Standard toolbar choose Data-Series in Columns or click on the **By Column** button.

4   Embed the chart and save the presentation.

5   Note that there are now labels on the x-axis (i.e. the horizontal axis).

Task 3: Improving chart appearance

Continuing from the previous task, we now seek to improve the general appearance of the chart.

Double-click on the chart to start Graph.

1   Delete the legend, which is now redundant, by clicking on it to select it, so that it is surrounded by black boxes. Press *Delete*.

2   We want to size the labels so that they fit on one line. First stretch the outer boundaries of the chart by dragging on the black box handles to ensure that the chart uses most of the space on the slide.

3   Next click on the x-axis to select it. Black boxes will appear to indicate that it is selected.

4   Choose Format-Selected Axes. This displays the Format Axis dialog box. Select the **Font** tab.

5   Change any characteristics that seem appropriate e.g. reduce the font size. Click on **OK**.

(!) Examine the chart to see whether the data labels now appear on one line. If they do not, try again!

We now want to insert the axis labels.

6   Choose Chart-Chart Options.

7   Click in the Category (X) Axis box in the Titles dialog box and type **Aerobic Activities**. Click on **OK**.

8   If this text is not selected (enclosed by a rectangle), click on it.

9   Choose Format-Font. Make the font Bold Italic.

(!) The chart may shrink during this process - simply stretch it again.

10 Repeat the process for the Z-axis, inserting the axis label **Number**.

Your chart should now resemble the chart displayed here.

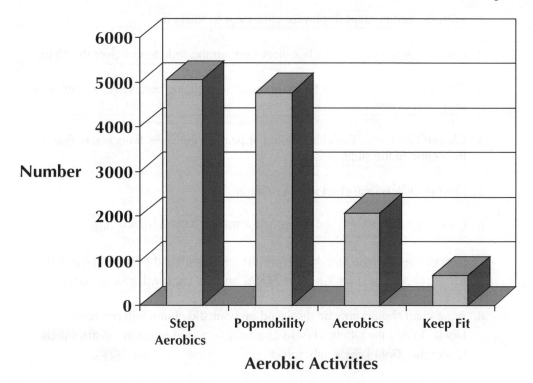

Changing the chart type

Graph offers a number of different 2-D and 3-D chart types. It is necessary to choose a chart type that effectively presents the data to be displayed. Once a chart type has been selected it may be necessary to undertake some formatting on the chart.

 You should select the chart type before applying any formatting.

Change the chart type as follows.

1 With an existing chart displayed in Graph, choose Chart-Chart Type. This will display the Chart Type dialog box.

2 Select an appropriate chart type. Click on **OK**.

3 Examine the chart produced and perform any necessary formatting.

Task 4: Chart type

This task uses the chart that you created earlier in this unit as a basis for a new chart. In other words, we experiment with displaying the same data in different ways. To do this we need first to make a copy of the earlier chart on a new slide and then to change the chart type of this new chart.

1 With the earlier chart displayed, click on it to select it.

2 Choose Edit-Copy-Chart. Click elsewhere on the slide to de-select the chart.

3 Choose Insert-New Slide. From the New Slide dialog box, select a blank or title only slide layout.

4 Choose Edit-Paste. The chart should appear on the slide. If necessary drag it to the centre of the slide.

5 Double click on the chart to enter Graph.

6 Choose Chart-Chart Type. This displays the Chart-Type dialog box.

7 Choose Pie from the Standard Types list and highlight the top left type in the Chart sub type section. Click on **OK** and the chart will change to this type.

8 A pie chart should now be displayed on your slide but it will not have any labels. To add the labels, choose Chart-Options and select the **Data Labels** tab. Under the **Data Labels** tab, select Show Percent. Click on **OK** .

9 Examine your chart. You may wish to stretch the chart, so that the pie is bigger. If the plot area of the chart has a border you can remove it by double-clicking on it and choosing None for the border.

10 The labels on the pie can be formatted further if you wish. Compare your original 3-D bar chart display and your pie chart display. Retain the one that you prefer, and delete the slide with the other display.

Task 5: A chart with two data series

As a separate one slide presentation, create a chart to compare attendance figures for two of the club's categories of membership: Junior and Junior Club over the period of five weeks shown below.

Week	Junior	Junior Club
22/3/98	12	30
29/3/98	13	39
5/4/98	8	3
12/4/98	23	59
19/4/98	29	63

Save this presentation as **Junior.**

Animating charts

Animation in slides will be considered in more detail in Unit 16, but a new feature in PowerPoint is the ability to animate elements of charts, so this will be considered here.

Animate a chart as follows.

1   Select the chart you want to animate.

2   Choose Slide Show-Custom Animation, and then select the **Chart Effects** tab.

3   Under Introduce chart elements, select how you want to animate the chart. The options in this list will depend on the type of chart selected.

4   Under Entry animation and sound, select the options you want. Use the Help pointer (click on **?** in the tool bar and point and click on the item you want more information on) or use the Office Assistant.

5   Click the **Timing** tab. To start the animation by clicking the chart, choose On mouse click. To start the animation automatically, choose Automatically, and then enter the number of seconds you want to elapse between the previous animation and the current one. The timing you set is also the time that will elapse between each animated element of the chart.

You can only use the animation effects on the **Chart Effects** tab, such as Wipe down, to animate an entire chart, not the elements of a chart. To use any of the animation effects, click the All at once option.

Task 6: Animating a chart

1   Open the presentation **Junior** and check that the data series are in rows. Select the chart (just click on it, don't double click as that will open Graph). Choose Slide Show-Custom Animation, and then select the **Chart Effects** tab.

2   Under Introduce chart elements choose by Element in Series. Remove the tick from the Animate grid and legend check box.

3   Under Entry animation and sound select Wipe Up. The default timing is On Mouse Click so just click on **OK** Go into Slide Show View and view the slide, clicking the mouse button to bring up each row of the graph.

4   Investigate what happens if you tick the Animate grid and legend check box. Save and close the presentation.

5   For further practise, add the following slide to the presentation **Briefing**, after the second slide. Experiment with animating it and save this presentation.

Good News on Sales

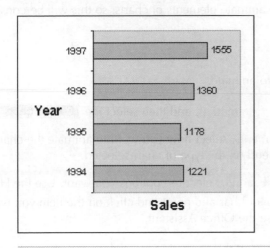

Using the drawing tools

What you will learn in this unit

PowerPoint allows you to create professional-looking images using its drawing features. The drawing tools enable you to add lines and shapes and customise them to suit your slide. When a line or shape is added to a slide it is known as an 'object'. By the end of this unit you will be able to:

■ create different drawing objects

■ select and edit drawing objects

■ choose colour, fill and rotation of drawing objects

■ align, group and ungroup drawing objects.

Creating drawing objects

To create drawing objects you will need to use the Drawing toolbar. If this toolbar is not displayed use View-Toolbars-Drawing to display it. As well as toolbar buttons this toolbar has several drop down menus so it offers a wide range of functions. These functions are listed in Quick Reference 2.

First, you must view the slide to which a drawing object is to be added in Slide View. All drawing objects, except freeforms, are created using the same technique. First select the tool which corresponds with the shape you wish to draw and then click and drag on the slide to create the object. Holding down the *Shift* key while dragging will produce squares rather than rectangles, circles rather than ellipses and horizontal or vertical lines. Holding down the *Ctrl* key while dragging will centre the object around your start point rather than your start point being the top left corner of the object's rectangle.

Creating standard shapes

Drawing Toolbar button	*Function*
Selection Tool	To select drawing objects that have already been created, click on this tool and then click on the object
Line Tool	For drawing lines
Rectangle Tool	For drawing rectangles or squares
Ellipse Tool	For drawing ellipses or circles
Free Rotate Tool	For rotating drawing objects freely
Auto Shapes	Generates a menu of shapes from which you may choose a shape

To save you drawing common shapes the Autoshapes menu offers a variety of shapes under several categories: Lines; Connectors; Basic Shapes; Block Arrows; Flowchart; Stars and Banners; Callouts; and Action Buttons. In each category is a sub-menu of choices. The sub-menu for Basic Shapes is illustrated here.

Choose the shape that you wish to add to your slide by selecting from a sub-menu. Drag on the slide to add the shape. Note that holding the *Shift* key while dragging will have the same effect as with the rectangle and ellipse tools.

Once a drawing object, however created, is added to a slide its size, position and characteristics may be altered. This will be explained in the following tasks.

Task 1: Adding drawing objects to a slide

1 Start a new presentation as a blank presentation and add a blank slide to it. This slide will be used for experimenting with the creation and deletion of drawing objects and will not be saved.

2 Add a rectangle, an ellipse and a line by clicking on the appropriate tool in turn and dragging the shape on the slide.

3 When you finish drawing each shape the pointer returns to being a selection pointer. You must therefore click on the tool again if you want to repeat the shape.

4 Select each object, by pointing to it and clicking, in turn and delete it by pressing the *Delete* key. When an object is selected it is bounded by sizing handles (small white boxes). Now, create a similar set of shapes, this time holding down the *Shift* key while dragging to create a square, a circle and a vertical or horizontal line.

Formatting shapes

If you add a shape other than a line to a slide, you will discover that it has a fill colour and an outside edge. You can change the colour of the fill and line either by using the **Fill Color** and **Line Color** buttons on the Drawing toolbar or by displaying the Format Autoshape dialog box. This dialog box, shown below, appears when you double click on the shape or you select the shape and choose Format-Autoshape.

If you format your shape to have No Fill and No Line you will no longer be able to see the object, although it will still be there!

To resize an object click on one of the sizing handles (if you point to one the pointer will change to a double-headed arrow) and drag. You can either drag a side or a corner. If your object is a line then you can drag either end. To move an object, click on it and drag. Avoid the sizing handles and check that the pointer is a four-headed arrow before you start dragging.

Some shapes also have a small yellow diamond. If you drag this you can modify the shape.

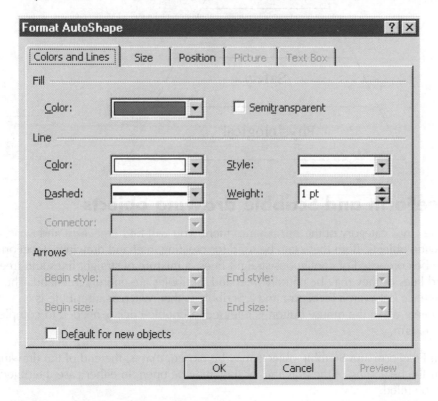

Task 2: Adding Autoshapes

In this task a slide showing Maslow's hierarchy (a diagram often used in studying motivation) will be created.

1   Start a new presentation as a blank presentation and add a blank slide to it. Open the Autoshapes menu, choose Basic Shapes and select the triangle shape. Holding down the *Shift* key while dragging create an isosceles triangle.

2 Click on the **Fill Color** button and select No fill. Size, by dragging a corner handle, and move the triangle to fill the slide. Add four lines to divide the triangle into five layers.

3 Drag a text box in each layer and add text as illustrated. Format and align this text. Save the presentation as **Maslow**.

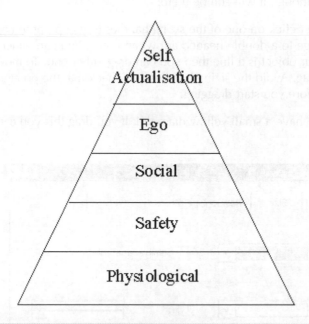

FreeForm and Scribble drawing objects

In the Lines category of the AutoShapes menu you will find FreeForm and Scribble drawing objects. Both these can be used for creating freehand drawings. FreeForms may be composed of contiguous straight lines, a mixture of straight lines and free-hand lines or they may be entirely freehand. Scribbles are entirely freehand. The difference between a FreeForm and a Scribble is that, whereas a scribble is complete when the mouse button is released, a double-click is needed to complete a FreeForm.

Both FreeForm and Scribble objects may be closed, that is, the end of the drawing joins the beginning of the drawing, or they may be open. In either case the object may be filled.

Draw a FreeForm object composed of straight lines as follows.

1 Select FreeForm from the AutoShapes Lines sub-menu. Click on the slide and release the mouse button. Point to where the line is to end and click. Repeat for as many joined lines as you require.

2 If you create an irregular polygon i.e. you join the end of the last line to the beginning of the first, then your FreeForm automatically finishes. If your aim is to create a regular polygon there may be one to suit in the Basic Shapes menu.

3 If you do not want to join the end to the beginning then double-click to signify that you have completed your FreeForm.

Draw a freehand FreeForm object as follows.

1 Select FreeForm from the AutoShapes Lines sub-menu. Click on the slide and drag; the pointer changes to a pencil shape while you are dragging.

2 If you finish at the same point that you started from then release the button and click once; otherwise double-click.

You may combine the two methods described to create a FreeForm object that is composed of straight and freehand lines.

Draw a freehand Scribble object as follows.

1 Select Scribble from the AutoShapes Lines sub-menu. Click on the slide and drag; the pointer changes to a pencil shape while you are dragging.

2 To finish release the mouse button. To create a closed shape finish at the start point.

Task 3: Creating FreeForm drawing objects

1 Start a new presentation as a blank presentation and add a blank slide to it. Click on the FreeForm tool and create a closed straight sided shape, an open straight sided shape, a closed freehand shape, and an open freehand shape.

2 Experiment with creating a shape that is composed of a mixture of straight and freehand lines.

3 Click on each one in turn and press *Delete*. Close without saving.

Editing freehand objects

As it is difficult to draw using the mouse, freehand drawings may be edited to remove the 'wobbles'. A freehand drawing is made up of a set of small curves (and lines if the object is a FreeForm with line sections) joined together. The point at which one curve or line joins another is known as a vertex (plural vertices) and vertices may be removed, added or moved. PowerPoint allows you to display these vertex handles and, by controlling them as described below, a freehand drawing can be re-worked to improve its appearance.

To	Do this
Display the vertex handles	Choose Draw-Edit Points on the Drawing toolbar. If you need to see the vertex handles more clearly, zoom in to the slide.
Move a vertex handle	Click on it and drag. When working with curves an extra handle appears that allows you to adjust the degree of curvature of the curve.

To	Do this
Delete a vertex handle	Hold down the _Ctrl_ key and click on it. The handle will be removed and the curve will join the two handles either side of the deleted one.
Add a vertex handle	Hold down the _Ctrl_ key and click anywhere on the line between two handles.

Once modifications to the drawing are complete click elsewhere on the slide and save your presentation.

Task 4 Editing FreeForm drawing objects

In this task some clouds of steam will be added to the 'Power Shower' text box in the slide created for **Advert** in Unit 9.

1   Open the presentation **Advert** and in Slide View display the text box slide.

2   Choose either the FreeForm or the Scribble drawing tool and draw a cloud of steam in the space above the 'Power Shower' text box. Make this shape a closed object i.e. finish in the same place as you started. Try to create another cloud using the other drawing tool (Scribble or FreeForm) to compare them. Don't worry if the result is not very pleasing as the shape will be edited.

3   Take the fill off by choosing No Fill from the Fill Color button menu.

4   Select a cloud to display the handles. If necessary, zoom in using the Zoom drop down list box on the standard toolbar.

5   Try dragging some of these handles to make your shape smoother.

6   Experiment with deleting and adding vertex handles. Experiment with adjusting the curvature of your curves.

7   Once you are satisfied with the end result click elsewhere on the slide. Save the presentation as **Advert**.

Fills and shadows

We have seen how to remove an object's fill and it is straightforward to choose a colour to fill an object. If you use the **Fill Color** button then you will be offered a choice of colours in keeping with the slide's colour scheme. Choosing More Fill Colors will let you choose from the spectrum of colours and choosing Fill Effects allows you to choose gradient shading or patterns for the shape.

The colour and style of the outside edge (line) of the object can be varied. The **Line Color** button allows you to select a colour for the outside edge and the **Line Style** and **Dash Style** buttons allow you to choose a style for the outside edge.

The object can be given a variety of shadow effects by choosing from the menu of shadow effects available from the **Shadow** button. Once a shadow has been applied to an object it can be manipulated using the Shadow Settings toolbar. To display the Shadow Settings toolbar, select the shadowed object and click on the **Shadow** button and choose Shadow Settings. Using this toolbar you can:

- switch the shadow on or off
- nudge the shadow up, down, left or right
- select the shadow colour.

Task 5: Fills and shadows

1 Continue from the last task. Select the cloud of steam and give this object a white fill by clicking on the **Fill Color** button in the Drawing toolbar. Using the **Line Color** button choose white for the line colour.

2 Use Copy and Paste to make copies of one of your cloud objects (so that you have three clouds) and move them to different parts of the slide (you may wish to overlap them or position them so that they overlap the text box).

3 Select one of the copies and investigate changing the colour, thickness and style of its edge. Finish by returning the line edge to its original setting.

4 Select one of the text boxes and investigate the choices available for its edge.

Rotation

To add to the variety of effects you can create, objects may be freely rotated. Text objects as well as drawing objects may be rotated. The Free Rotate tool allows you to rotate an object about its centre by any angle you desire. You may rotate an object as follows.

1   Select the object. Click on the Free Rotate button. The pointer changes shape to include the free rotate symbol and circular green rotation handles appear around the object.

2   Click on a rotation handle of the selected object and drag to rotate the object around its centre.

Task 6: Rotating an object

1   Select one of the clouds of steam and rotate it by clicking on the Free Rotate tool on the Drawing toolbar and dragging one of the rotation handles of the object.

2   To finish this slide, using the arrow button, draw four arrows on the slide starting at the centre box and pointing one to each of the other text boxes.

Draw one arrow, double click on it and apply the thickness and size of arrow-head of your choice, then copy and paste it, repositioning each copy.

3   Save the presentation.

Aligning and grouping drawing objects

PowerPoint provides guides or the Draw-Align or Distribute command to align objects horizontally or vertically. The Align command aligns two or more objects relative to each other either to the left, to the right, to the horizontal centre, to the top, to the bottom, or to the vertical centre. The guides align an individual object or group of objects to a vertical or horizontal straight edge. To make this alignment exact use the Draw-Snap-To Grid feature i.e. the To Grid button in the menu is depressed. Objects can then only be placed (snapped to) an invisible grid.

You may align objects using the guides.

1   Point to a blank area of your slide and click the right mouse button. Choose Guides from the shortcut menu that appears. Vertical and horizontal dotted lines appear in the middle of the slide; these are the guides. The keyboard shortcut to display these guides is *Ctrl+g*.

2   The guides may be moved to different positions by dragging. As you drag, a guide indicator shows the distance you are from the centre of the slide. For accurate guide positioning you may find it better to turn off the Snap to Grid feature.

3 Once the guides are positioned, select and drag objects and position them using the guides. The guides can be hidden using the shortcut menu as described in Step 1.

You may align objects using the Align command.

1 Select all the objects you wish to align. Select more than one object by holding down the *Shift* key while clicking on each object in turn.

2 Choose Draw-Align or Distribute. A sub-menu appears in which you can select the type of alignment required, for example, Align Middle. The objects will align according to the alignment selected. Don't forget the Undo command if the effect is not what you anticipated.

Objects may be grouped together, ungrouped, and regrouped to make editing and moving easier. In Task 8 below, a stick figure is created from several line objects and a circle object and, by grouping these, the stick figure can be moved and resized without having to operate on each object individually.

To group objects, select all the objects you wish to group either by selecting each in turn while holding down the *Shift* key, or by dragging a selection box to enclose all the objects you wish to group. Their handles will appear. Choose Draw-Group; there will now be only one set of handles surrounding the grouped object.

To ungroup objects, select the grouped object; choose Draw-Ungroup. All objects making up the group are now shown each with their own sizing handles. Click outside the selection rectangle to de-select the objects.

To regroup a previously grouped set of objects, select one of the objects that belong to the group and choose Draw-Regroup.

 When working with objects you may wish to layer them in a particular order. The commands for layering can be found in Unit 10.

Task 7: Using the guides, aligning objects

1 Continue working with the slide used in the last task.

2 Point to a blank area of your slide, click the right mouse button and choose Guides from the shortcut menu.

3 Drag the vertical guide to line up with the left edge of the 'Power Shower' text box.

4 Move the clouds of steam objects and align them with the vertical guide.

5 Try moving the horizontal guide and aligning the objects horizontally. If you wish you may save these changes.

6   Select all the clouds of steam by holding down the *Shift* key as you make each selection.

7   Choose Draw-Align and Distribute and experiment with the different types of alignment that you can apply to your objects. Close the presentation.

Task 8: Grouping objects

In this task a logo for Chelmer Leisure and Recreation Centre will be created.

1   Start a new presentation and add a blank slide. The aim is to create the logo illustrated.

2   The text can be created by using WordArt and the outer rectangle by using the rounded corner rectangle tool (in the Autoshapes menu).

3   The stick figure is created using a circle and lines. Create a stick figure that is larger than you will eventually want. It is easier to see what you are doing and you will see how to make the figure smaller later in this task.

4   When you have created all the objects composing the stick figure, select them all and choose Draw-Group.

5   Only one set of handles will now appear. Experiment with using these to re-size the stick figure. You may wish to experiment with copying the figure and ungrouping the grouped object.

6   Save the finished slide as a presentation called **Logo1**.

Task 9: Adding a logo to a slide master

1   Open the presentation **Advert** and display the Slide Master.

2   In the **Logo1** presentation, group all the objects in the logo together. Select and copy the logo, using Edit-Copy.

3   Using the Window menu switch to the Slide Master of **Advert.** Use Edit-Paste to
    add the logo to the master. Size and position the logo in the bottom right corner,
    then close the Master.

4   Go into Slide Show View and note how the logo appears on every slide. If you
    wish to remove this master object from an individual slide, display the slide in
    question, choose Format-Background and check the Omit background graphics
    from Master check box.

5   Save and display the presentation.

Importing and exporting

What you will learn in this unit

Importing in a Windows environment is generally achieved by copying from one application and pasting into another application. This is an extension of the use of Copy and Paste that is used in one presentation. Copy and Paste may be used to copy one or more slides from a presentation and to copy them into another presentation.

If text and charts have already been created by another application then these may be copied into a presentation. The copy may be linked to the original so that if changes are made to the original then the copy can be updated to reflect the changes.

By the end of this unit you will be able to:

- copy slides from one presentation to another
- import word processed text and tables
- import spreadsheet data and charts
- export a presentation outline to a word processor
- put existing text into a table.

The tasks in this unit assume that you have available Word 97 and Excel 97.

Importing slides between presentations

You may find that you create one or more slides that you might wish to use in other presentations. There is no need to re-create these slides as they may be copied from one presentation to another. Copy slides as follows.

1 View the presentation containing the slides you wish to copy in Slide Sorter View.

2 Select the slide or slides you wish to copy. Choose Edit-Copy or click on the Copy button. The slides are now copied to the Clipboard.

3 Open the presentation to which you wish to add the copied slides. In Slide Sorter View position the insertion point where the slide or slides are to be inserted and choose Edit-Paste or click on the Paste button in the toolbar. Save the presentation.

Slides pasted into a presentation take on the characteristics of the presentation they have been pasted into. This means that you may copy slides from a presentation designed for conversion to overhead projection into one designed for an on screen presentation without having to edit the characteristics of the new slides.

Task 1: Copying slides from one presentation to another

1   Open the presentation **Project** in Slide Sorter View.

2   Select any slide. Choose Edit-Copy.

3   Open the presentation **Facility** in Slide Sorter View. Position the insertion point at a point where you think this slide should be.

4   Choose Edit-Paste to copy the selected slide. Save and view the presentation. Note that the slide has taken on the characteristics of the **Facility** presentation.

Importing word processed text and tables

Text and tables created using a Windows word processor can be copied and pasted into a PowerPoint slide. The copy may be linked to the original so that changes in it will be reflected in the presentation. This is useful for keeping presentations up-to-date with current information.

You may find that, although you can create and add borders to a table in Word, the borders do not come across properly into PowerPoint. It is possible that there might be a bug fix to resolve this in the future, but at the present time it does not work as it should.

You may import text and tables from Word as follows.

1   Create the text and/or table using Word.

2   Select and copy it. Switch to or start PowerPoint and open the presentation to which the selected text is to be added.

3   In Slide View, display the slide to which you wish to add the text.

4   You may paste your selection into a text box, in which case it takes on the characteristics of the slide. Apply any formatting to the text in the slide.

5   If you paste the copied text directly into the slide it will be a Word object and you will need to double click on it to edit it in a Word environment.

You may link text and tables from Word to a slide as follows.

1   Select the text as before and copy it. Switch to or start PowerPoint and open the presentation to which the selected text is to be added.

2   In Slide View, display the slide to which you wish to add the text. Use Edit-Paste Special and in the Paste Special dialog box choose the Paste Link option. This will automatically update the slide whenever the text in Word is changed.

Task 2: Importing a Word table

This task requires Word.

1 In Word create the following table:

Week	Junior	Junior Club
22/3/98	*12*	*30*
29/3/98	*13*	*39*
5/4/98	*8*	*3*
12/4/98	*23*	*59*
19/4/98	*29*	*63*

2 Select it and copy it using Edit-Copy. Switch to PowerPoint. Open the presentation **Junior**.

3 Create a new blank slide. Use Edit-Paste to copy the selected text onto the slide.

4 Drag a corner handle to make the table larger. You may wish to refer back to Unit 8 for other aspects of table formatting.

5 Create another blank slide and this time use Edit-Paste Special and set the Paste Link option. Format the table. Save the presentation.

6 Switch to Word and change *63* to *57*.

7 Switch back to PowerPoint and you should find that after a few moments the change is reflected in this slide but not the others.

If you have added borders and shading to the table they may not be displayed on the slide.

Task 3: Copying and pasting text from Word

The slide entitled **Topics of Discussion** in the presentation **Project** needs updating. Some text to be added to this slide will be created in Word and then copied to the presentation.

1 In Word create a new document containing the following text:

Usage of Facilities

Preferred Configuration

Atlanta Sports Proposal

Summary and Recommendations

2 In PowerPoint open the presentation **Project** in Outline View.

3 Using Copy and Paste, and switching between PowerPoint and Word, edit the **Topics of Discussion** slide to read:

  ◆ *Chelmer Leisure Centre*

  ◆ *Usage of Facilities*

  ◆ *Preferred Configuration*

  ◆ *Atlanta Sports Proposal*

  ◆ *Summary and Recommendations*

4 Save the presentation **Project**. View the presentation.

Importing spreadsheet data and charts

Data and charts created using a Windows spreadsheet can be copied and pasted into a PowerPoint slide. The copy may be linked to the original so that changes in it will be reflected in the presentation.

You may import data and charts from Excel as follows.

1 Create the data and/or chart using Excel.

2 Select and copy it. Switch to or start PowerPoint and open the presentation to which the selected text is to be added.

3 In Slide View, display the slide to which you wish to add the text.

4 Paste your selection into the slide where it becomes an Excel Object. It may be edited by double clicking on it to invoke an Excel environment.

You may link data and charts from Excel to a slide as follows.

1 Select the data/chart as before and copy it. Switch to or start PowerPoint and open the presentation to which the selected data/chart is to be added.

2 In Slide View, display the slide to which you wish to add the data/chart. Use Edit-Paste Special and in the Paste Special dialog box choose the Paste Link option. This will automatically update the slide whenever the data in Excel is changed.

Task 4: Importing an Excel spreadsheet

This task requires Excel.

1 In Excel enter the data from Task 2 (you may copy it from Word). Make sure that all the data is visible in the cell. If necessary, drag a column line to make the column wider.

2 Select the data and copy it using Edit-Copy. Switch to PowerPoint. Open the presentation **Junior**.

3 Add a new blank slide. Use Edit-Paste to copy the selected data. Drag a corner handle to enlarge the cells. Drag the object to position it on the slide.

4 Switch back to Excel and create a chart using this data. Select this chart and copy it using Edit-Copy. Switch to PowerPoint. Use Edit-Paste to copy the selected chart. The chart may be re-sized and moved to a suitable position on the slide. Double click on the chart to select it. Click on Format-Select Chart Area to display the Format Chart Area dialog box. Click on a colour that compliments the colour of the slide outside the chart. Click **OK** .

5 Add another blank slide and this time use Edit-Paste Special and set the Paste Link option. Repeat for the data. See if you can arrange both chart and data on the slide.

6 Switch to Excel and change *63* to *57* as in the previous task.

7 Switch back to PowerPoint and you should find that after a few moments the change is reflected in both the data and the chart on this slide.

Exporting a presentation outline to Word

PowerPoint has a Report It feature which allows the outline of a presentation to be exported directly into Word. Although you may print a presentation in Outline View there may be occasions when you want the added features of a word-processor to edit the outline, for example, to prepare it for inclusion in a report.

You may export a presentation outline to Word as follows.

1 Open the presentation. Choose File-Send To-Microsoft Word. This will display the Write-Up dialog box. Choose one of the options in Page Layout in Word, click on **OK** . The slides should appear as part of a Word document.

2 Edit the presentation outline as you would a Word document.

Note that even the slides can be edited but that you will need to double click on them first.

Task 5: Exporting a presentation to Word

For this task you will need both PowerPoint and Word.

1 Open the presentation **Project**. Choose File-Send To-Microsoft Word, then choose Notes next to Slides in the Write-Up dialog box. Click on **OK** . PowerPoint starts or switches to Word and inserts the slides with the title text and main text format into a new Word document.

2 Format as appropriate, save, and print the Word document.

Exporting tab separated text to Word for conversion to a table

As noted in Unit 8 if you create a slide with two or more columns of text separated by tabs then PowerPoint does not offer a 'convert text to table' facility. The following task exports some tab separated text to Word, converts it to a table, and then re-imports it. When PowerPoint exports text it tends to reduce the font size so, as you intend to re-import it, note the font size of the slide text before starting.

Task 6: Exporting a table to Word

For this task you will need Word.

1   Open the presentation **Advert** and display the slide **Fitness Suite Passcards**.

2   Select the last part of the slide showing the prices. Use Edit-Cut to remove it to the clipboard.

3   Switch to Word, start a new document and use Edit-Paste. Select the pasted text and use Table-Convert text to table. Choose the number of columns for the table.

4   Select the table, switch back to PowerPoint, de-select the text box (click at the edge of the slide) and use Edit-Paste.

5   The table will need some editing so double-click on it and adjust alignment, font and colour and add borders as desired. Remember, the borders formatting does not always work correctly in PowerPoint. Finally click on the slide to embed the table and drag to the desired position on the slide. Save.

Slide transitions and Autorunning presentations

What you will learn in this unit

If you are giving an on-screen slide show, you can use a mouse click to advance through the slides. When you move from one slide to the next this is known as a transition. PowerPoint provides a number of transition effects that you can apply.

To exercise more control over the order in which the slides are displayed you can use action buttons or the shortcut menu that appears if you click the right hand mouse button during a presentation.

If you are not going to be present to advance the slides, then you can create an autorunning presentation. An autorunning presentation is one which runs by itself, i.e. the slides advance automatically. Autorunning presentations can be set to loop continuously, the first slide following the last.

Autorunning presentations are suitable for advertising, such as at a trade fair where a stand may not be manned continuously or customers can have their attention held while the sales personnel are busy. Autorunning presentations need to be under computer control and so are only suitable for on-screen or other computer display. Additionally a commentary or narration can be added to give an extra dimension to the presentation.

By the end of this unit you will be able to:

- select slide transition effects
- add action buttons to presentations
- set the length of time for which a slide is displayed
- make an autorunning presentation
- edit slide transitions
- add narration to a presentation.

Slide transitions and timings

When the presentation moves from one slide to the next this is known as a transition. The length of time a slide remains on screen is known as the slide timing.

A transition from one slide to the next can simply be that the next slide just appears. However, to add interest, the way in which the next slide appears can be chosen. For example, a series of checker (chess) board squares can move across the screen changing the previous slide to the next one in the presentation. PowerPoint provides a variety of transition effects from which you can choose. However, it is good practice to use only one type of transition throughout a presentation.

Slide transitions are selected while you are working with your presentation in Slide Sorter View. You may apply a transition as follows.

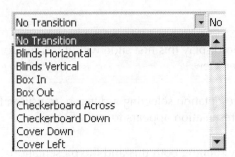

1   In Slide Show View Select the slide or slides to which the transition is to be applied.

2   Open the Transition Effect drop down list box on the left side of the Slide Sorter toolbar.

3   Scroll to the transition you require and click on it to select it. A transition symbol appears below the left hand corner of the selected slide or slides.

4   To see a slide with the transition, select it and click on the **Slide Show** button. Press the *Esc* key to return to Slide Sorter View. Repeat for all slides in the presentation for which you wish to set a transition.

 If all the slides in the presentation are to have the same transition then they can all be selected before the transition is chosen. To select all slides in Slide Sorter view choose Edit-Select All. If a selected set of slides is to have the same transition, hold down the *Shift* key while selecting the slides and then select the transition.

Task 1: Choosing a slide transition

1   Display the presentation **Advert** in Slide Sorter View.

2   Choose Edit-Select All to select all the slides, open the Transition effect drop down list box and select Checkerboard Across.

3   Click on the **Slide Show** button and view the presentation to see the effect of using this transition. You will be returned to the Slide Sorter View on completion of the presentation. Press *Esc* if you want to return to Slide Sorter View before the end of the presentation.

4   Save the presentation.

Task 2: Choosing individual slide transitions

1 Display the presentation **Advert 1** in Slide Sorter View.

2 Select the first slide, open the Transition effect drop down list box and select a transition of your choice.

3 Click on the **Slide Show** button to display this first slide with this transition. Press *Esc* to return to the Slide Sorter View.

4 Repeat for the other slides in the presentation selecting a different transition for each slide in such a way that the presentation appears to gather speed.

5 Save the presentation. You could try running both this and the presentation **Advert** to consider whether single or mixed transitions are more appropriate for this presentation when used in the entrance foyer of a Leisure Centre.

Action buttons

An action button is a button that you can place on a slide. When the slide show is being presented, the action associated with that button will take place when the button is clicked. Here we will consider the middle row of action buttons, illustrated below; some of the other buttons will be considered in Unit 18.

In the middle row of the set of action buttons are **Back or Previous**, **Forward or Next**, **Beginning** and **End**. Their effects are to move back one slide, move forward one slide, move to the first slide and move to the last slide, respectively.

To add one of these buttons, in Slide View, click on Slide Show – Action Buttons and then point to the slide and drag out the button to the approximate size required. If you would like the button to be available on all the slides then add the button to the Slide Master.

Task 3: Adding slide navigation action buttons to a slide master

In this task the action buttons that move to the beginning, end, previous and next slides will be added to the Slide Master of the presentation **Project**.

1 Open the presentation **Project** in Slide view. Using View-Master-Slide Master display the Slide Master.

2   Choose Slide Show-Action Buttons and click on Action Button: Back or Previous. Click on the slide and the button will appear on the screen followed by the Action Settings dialog box. Click on OK . Do not worry about size or position as this will be dealt with subsequently. Note that alternatively you can choose this action button from the Autoshapes menu on the Drawing toolbar.

3   Repeat this process to add the Forward or Next , Beginning and End buttons. Do not worry at this stage about size or position. Once you have added all four buttons then you can make them all the same size. To do this, select all the buttons (hold down *Shift* key while clicking on each button in turn), choose Format-Autoshape and select the Size tab. In the Height box specify, say 1cm and in the Width box specify, say, 1.25cm. Click on OK .

4   Drag the date area to another place on the Master, say the top of the slide, and roughly position the buttons in the bottom left corner. Arrange them in the order Beginning , Previous , Next and End .

5   To align the buttons, select them all and use Draw-Align or Distribute-Align top. To space them out neatly use Draw-Align or Distribute-Distribute horizontally. To be able to move them all as one, while they are all still selected use Draw-Group to group the buttons. The result should look something like the buttons illustrated.

6   Save the presentation and view it in Slide Show View, trying out the slide navigation buttons. If you wish, you can remove the buttons from the fitness suite diagram slide, if it looks too cluttered. To do this, select this slide in Slide Sorter View, choose Format-Background and tick the Omit background graphics from master check box and click on Apply .

7   Save, view and close this presentation.

Slide show shortcut menu

The slide show shortcut menu appears if you press the right hand mouse button during a presentation. It allows you to move back or forwards one slide or to go to a specific slide number. To go to a particular slide, choose Go-Slide Navigator and the Slide Navigator dialog box will allow you to choose the slide to go to.

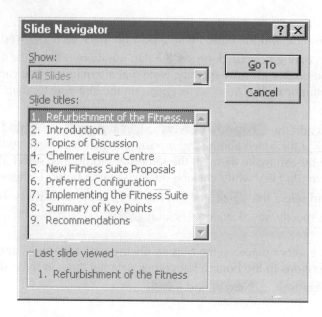

Slide timings

If you are not sure of the length of transition times to set between slides, because you don't know how long it will take your audience to read them, then you may rehearse the slide show and set the timing as you run it.

 Read the following instructions before trying the task below.

1   In Slide Sorter View, open the presentation for which you wish to rehearse the transition times.

2   Click on the **Rehearse Timing** button 🖰 on the Slide Sorter toolbar. The slide show begins, displaying a Rehearsal dialog box in the lower right corner of the screen. This box shows the time the current slide is to be displayed, and the total elapsed time is shown running.

3   Read and view the slide and when you feel that adequate time has elapsed click on the forward button to move to the next slide.

4   Repeat this process for each slide in the presentation.

5   At the end of the presentation a dialog box appears informing you of the total time for the slide show. Click on   **Yes**   to save the new time settings.

6   You will be asked if you wish to review the timings in Slide Sorter View. If you wish to amend any timings then see the 'Editing transitions' section below.

Autorunning presentations

Once timings have been assigned to slides, irrespective of transition types, the slide show can be set to run continuously until the *Esc* key is pressed. To make a presentation into an autorunning presentation: choose Slide Show-Set up Show, and to make the slide show loop continuously, tick the Loop continuously until 'Esc' check box in the Setup Show dialog box. The slide show will loop until the *Esc* key is pressed.

Task 4: Rehearsing slide transition times

In this task the transition times for the presentation **Advert** will be rehearsed.

1   Open the presentation **Advert** in Slide Sorter View. Click on the   **Rehearse Timing**   button on the Slide Sorter toolbar.

2   Read and view the slide and when you feel that adequate time has elapsed click on the   ▷   button to move to the next slide.

3   Repeat for all the slides in the presentation. Save the time settings and save the presentation. View the presentation, and you should see your timings coming into effect.

4   To make the slide show loop continuously, choose Slide show-Setup Show and tick the Loop continuously until 'Esc' check box.

5   View the slide show which will loop until the *Esc* key is pressed.

Editing transitions and timings

You may return to a presentation and revise the type and timing of slides in that presentation. The   **Transition**   button in the Slide Sorter toolbar will display the Transition dialog box, through which you can see the existing settings and modify them if you wish.

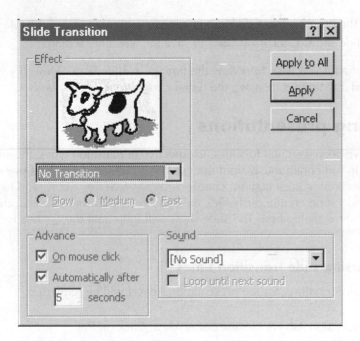

Task 5: Editing transitions

1   Open the presentation **Advert** in Slide Sorter View. Select one of the slides.

2   Click on the **Transition** button 🖅 and review the settings in the dialog box.

Experiment with altering the transitions and timings for slides, viewing each set of changes.

3   When you are satisfied with the result save the presentation.

Adding narration to a slide show

If you are creating an autorunning presentation then you may wish to add audio narration and other sound effects to your presentation. If you are making your slide show available on the Internet then narration may be a useful aid, but it is best to keep sound clips short as they take a long time to download.

To record a narration, your computer needs a sound card and a microphone. Generally you would record a narration before you run the slide show, but it can be recorded during the presentation. If you do not want narration throughout the entire slide show, you can also record separate sounds or comments on selected slides or objects.

⊘   If you decide to change something in the narration that you have recorded, you will need to delete the entire narration and rerecord it. Because voice narration takes precedence over all other sounds, if you are running a slide show that includes both narration and other sounds, only the narration will be played.

You may record a voice narration as follows.

1   Choose Slide Show-Record Narration. A dialog box appears showing the amount
    of free disk space and the number of minutes that you can record.

2   To insert the narration on your slides as an embedded object (the recording is
    saved as part of the presentation file) and to begin recording, click OK . To
    insert the narration as a linked object (the recording is saved in a separate file),
    select the Link narrations in check box, and then click OK to begin
    recording.

3   When the slide show starts add narration as you advance through it slide by
    slide.

 You do not need to record narration for every slide; simply move on past those
    slides without narration.

4   At the end of the show, you are asked whether to save the timings along with the
    narration. If you do, choose Yes , otherwise, to save only the narration,
    choose No .

5   In Slide View you will see a Sound icon   appears in the lower-right
    corner of each slide that has narration.

When you run the slide show, the narration will automatically play with the show.
To run the slide show without narration, choose Slide Show-Set Up Show and tick
the Show without narrations check box. Because you cannot record and play
sounds at the same time, while you are recording you will not hear other sounds
that you may have inserted in your slide show.

To remove narration from a slide, display the slide in Slide View, select the Sound
icon and delete it by pressing *Delete*.

A specific task is not given here but if you do have multimedia capabilities then
make a copy of the presentation **Project** and experiment with adding narration, for
example, by recording the slide titles.

Animation

What you will learn in this unit

In on-screen presentations, you may wish to display bullet points on a slide one at a time, or even make different objects appear progressively. These features use slide animation. There are many different animation effects from which you can choose, and in addition you can set timings for these animation events. By the end of this unit you will be able to:

■ animate bullet points

■ create custom animation of slide objects.

In this unit we demonstrate typical uses of animation in professional presentations. You may also like to investigate the potential for using animations to create humourous and special effects.

Animated slides

An animated slide (also called a progressive disclosure slide or build slide) is one where each bullet point in the main text appears independently of the others. Use an animated slide when you want to reveal bullet points one at a time. Further, you can set up the way you want each point to appear (to fly in from the left, for instance) and whether you want the other points already on the slide to dim when a new point is added. Similar animation effects can be extended to other slide objects, such as slide titles, graphics and charts.

Text preset animation

In Slide Sorter View animation can be easily added to a slide (or slides) using the Text Preset Animation list in the Slide Sorter toolbar.

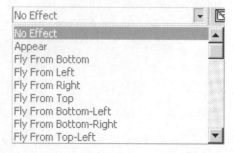

Select the slide or slides to which animation is to be added and choose the type of animation you require from the drop down list.

When choosing animation effects it is better to use either the same effect throughout the presentation or a very small variety of effects. (This of course assumes that your aim is not to confuse or unduly excite your audience!)

Preset text animation is also available through the **Slide Show-Preset Animation** command. This provides a different set of animations which include sound effects as well as animation effects.

Task 1: Adding text preset animation

1   Open the presentation **Briefing** and display it in Slide Sorter View.

2   Select the slide entitled **Overview**, open the Text Preset Animation drop down list on the Slide Sorter toolbar, and choose the effect Zoom out slightly.

3   Select the slide entitled **Computer Training** and choose another animation effect. View the slide show. If you have a sound card and speakers then use Slide Show-Slide Transition to select a sound effect, for example, Laser, from the list available through this command.

4   Return to Slide Sorter View and experiment with the use of other animation effects for bullet points on other slides in this presentation.

5   View the presentation as a slide show, using View-Slide Show.

6   Save and close this presentation.

 Note that first level bullets are treated individually for animation, but lower levels normally animate as a group.

Customising animation effects

Further enhancements to animation can be made using the Slide Show-Custom Animation command, available in Slide View. The Custom Animation dialog box appears as illustrated on the following page.

Through this dialog box it is possible to animate other objects on a slide in addition to bulleted text. When the dialog box opens the **Timing** tab is selected. Through this section you can choose which objects are to be animated. You choose the order in which the objects are animated and whether the object is animated when you click the mouse or after a certain length of time. In the dialog box overleaf there are two objects on the slide, one of which, the text, is animated while the other, the slide title, is not animated.

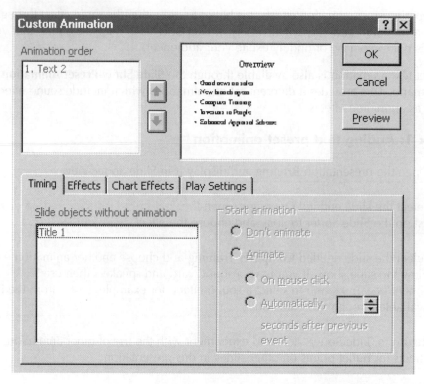

In the Effects section, as illustrated below, you can select the desired animation and sound effects. If you want a point to dim and change colour as the next point appears, open the After animation drop down list box. You can select a colour from

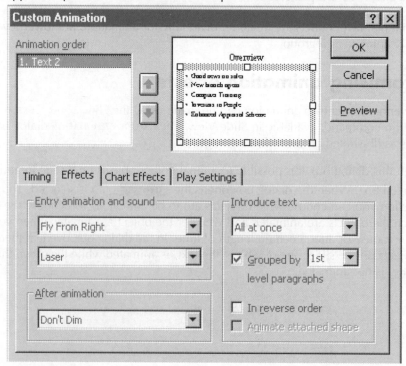

those suggested or opt for a wider choice of colours or even choose to hide the object after animation. You can select how the text should appear, either all at once or word by word or letter by letter.

 Only choose letter by letter text appearance for small pieces or text, say one or two words.

When you have set the animation you require click on **OK** and view the result.

Task 2: Creating slides with custom animation

In this task we will explore some custom effects that can be applied to text objects in slides.

1   Open the presentation **Project** and display it in Slide View.

2   Select the slide entitled **Topics for Discussion**. Choose Slide Show-Custom Animation.

3   Under the **Timing** tab, select the Text 2 object and choose Animate and On mouse click.

4   Under the **Effects** tab, choose Spiral for entry animation. Choose Whoosh for entry sound, if you have a sound card.

5   Open the After animation drop down list and choose one of the eight suggested colours. The text will become this colour when a new point is introduced.

6   View the effect and save the presentation. Experiment with adding animation effects of your own to other bulleted slides in this presentation, remembering that for actual presentations you would want to place importance on consistency and harmony in animation effects, both visually and aurally.

7   Open the presentation **Advert** and add animation effects to slides that have bullet points. As this is an autorunning presentation, the animation effects help to guide the reader through the slide and to keep their attention. Under the **Timings** tab set times for the animation. View the presentation and adjust the length of time between points so that there is time to read each point as it is presented. When you are satisfied with the result save this presentation.

Task 3: Animating other slide objects

This task will explore some effects that can be applied to non-text objects on slides.

1   Open the presentation **Project** and display it in Slide View.

2   Select the slide **Atlanta Sports Proposal**. This slide has a table embedded in it. Choose Slide Show-Custom Animation. Under the **Timing** tab, select the Object 1 (the table) and choose Animate and On mouse click. Under the **Effects** tab, choose Wipe Down for entry animation.

3   Move to the slide **Atlanta Site Plan** and try adding an effect to the image, such as Vertical Blinds Across.

4   View the effects and save the presentation.

Dos and Don'ts of animation

1   Don't use too many different animation effects in one presentation.

2   If you choose different effects then try to harmonise these, say, by choosing effects of a similar nature e.g. Wipe Up, Wipe Down.

3   If you add sound to an effect then consider how it will affect the flow of the speaker's narrative. If the presentation is autorunning then you may wish to choose something that would gain a viewer's attention but not their ridicule. Again, harmonise any audio effects that you add; an audience is likely to find continual beeps or whooshes irritating.

4   Use Timings for autorunning presentations and try to set the length of time each point or slide is displayed to be just long enough for the viewer to digest the information presented. If Timings are used with presentations or selected slides in a presentation given 'live' by a speaker then rehearse carefully so that they work as intended.

5   Choose letter by letter or word by word animation sparingly and only for objects with small amounts of text.

6   If you change the colour of a bullet point when the next is animated, choose a colour that harmonises with the slide colour scheme and blends in to the background more than the active point.

7   Animation at the beginning of a presentation can help to engage the audience's attention but repeating effects thereafter can easily lose it.

8   Think about the content of the presentation, the context in which it is being delivered and the type of audience when choosing animation effects, both visual and audio. An autorunning presentation at a trade fair will differ from one given at a monthly sales meeting, which in turn will differ from a talk on your hobby given to an interested community group.

Organisational charts

What you will learn in this unit

An organisational chart is one that is used to show the structure of an organisation. These structures are hierarchical with, say, a managing director at the top level with each succeeding level representing a lower level of management. As there are generally more managers at the lower levels then this chart takes on a 'root-like' (upside-down tree) structure. An example of a simple structure is shown below.

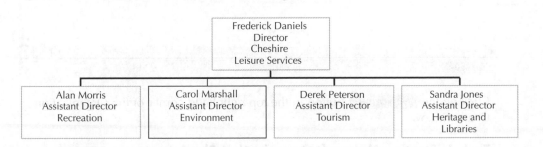

Cheshire Leisure - Management Structure

By the end of this unit you will be able to:

- create a simple organisational chart
- enter text into chart boxes
- create additional boxes on the chart
- edit an organisational chart.

Starting Microsoft Organization Chart

To enable you to produce professional organisational charts PowerPoint uses an application called Microsoft Organization Chart. This application is used to create the chart which is embedded into a slide when complete. An embedded Organizational Chart may be revisited later if editing is required.

To start Microsoft Organization Chart, either

- choose an Organization Chart Layout from the New Slide dialog box and double-click on the Organization Chart placeholder

or

- in Slide View, choose Insert-Picture-Organization Chart.

The Organization Chart application starts with a default chart displayed.

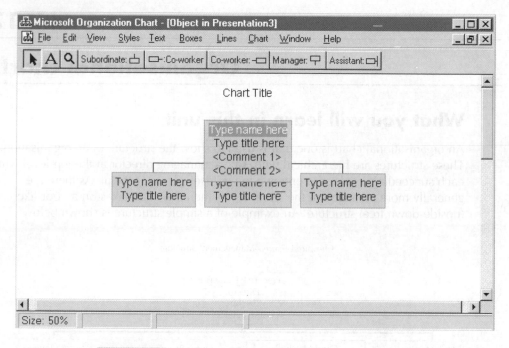

Click on the **Maximize** button in the top right hand corner of the Organization Chart window.

Task 1: Starting Microsoft Organization Chart

1   Start a new presentation as a blank presentation and choose Organization Chart Layout from the Slide Autolayout dialog box. Double-click on the Organization Chart placeholder.

2   Click on the **Maximize** button of the Organization Chart window.

Selecting and entering information into chart boxes

Before any editing or reformatting of chart boxes can be performed the box or boxes must be selected. When the default chart loads the top level box is selected and appears highlighted.

To	Do this
Select one box	Click on the box
Select a set of boxes	Drag a selection rectangle around the boxes
Select the whole chart	Choose Edit-Select-All
Select one level of the chart	Choose Edit-Select and, for example, **All Managers**, **Branch**, or **Lowest Level**.

Table 17.1

With a chart box selected, text may be entered. When the box is clicked a larger text box appears with the following placeholders:

Type name here
Type title here
<Comment 1>
<Comment 2>

To alter the placeholder text highlight it by clicking and dragging and then type in the required text. The comment lines are optional and can be ignored. When the text has been added click on a blank part of the screen to add the box into the chart.

Task 2: Altering text in chart boxes

This task continues from Task 1 and investigates selecting and entering text into the organisational chart boxes.

1 To note the appearance of a selected box, click one of the four boxes in the default chart to select it. Click on another box to select that. Finally select the top level box.

2 Double-click on the selected top level box to display the text box. Select each text placeholder and replace it with

Frederick Daniels

Director

Cheshire

Leisure Services

3 Now click on a blank part of the screen.

4 Repeat the process for the other lower level boxes adding the following people to the chart: *Alan Morris, Assistant Director, Recreation; Carol Marshall, Assistant Director, Environment;* and *Derek Peterson, Assistant Director, Tourism.*

5 In the same way edit the Chart Title (select then type) to read: *Management Structure.*

Embedding the organisational chart into the slide

When the organisation chart is complete, it can be embedded into the slide and the presentation saved. As you need to embed the chart before saving it may be useful to do this before the chart is complete. An embedded chart can easily be re-opened for editing by double-clicking on it.

To embed a chart into a slide use File-Exit and Return to Presentation. Answer
Yes to the Update object in presentation dialog box.

Task 3: Embedding and re-opening an organisational chart

Continue from the previous task.

1   Choose File-Exit and Return to Presentation and click on **Yes** to update the chart in the presentation..

2   Add the title *Cheshire Leisure Services* to the slide and save the presentation as **Orgchart**.

Adding and deleting chart boxes

The default organisational chart is unlikely to have the structure that you require and you will wish to modify it by adding and removing boxes and levels. In this activity we shall concentrate on simple structure charts and use the buttons on the Organization toolbar to create such charts. These buttons are summarised in Table 17.2.

Button

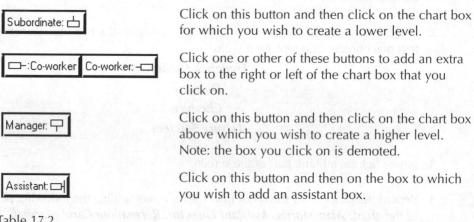

Subordinate:	Click on this button and then click on the chart box for which you wish to create a lower level.
:Co-worker Co-worker:	Click one or other of these buttons to add an extra box to the right or left of the chart box that you click on.
Manager:	Click on this button and then click on the chart box above which you wish to create a higher level. Note: the box you click on is demoted.
Assistant:	Click on this button and then on the box to which you wish to add an assistant box.

Table 17.2

Deleting boxes - select box and delete it by pressing the *Delete* key. Note if a box is deleted which has subordinate levels then these are not deleted, they move up one level.

To cater for more variety in a chart, different group styles may be chosen from the Styles menu. An example of a vertical group style can be seen in the chart illustrated in Task 6.

Task 4: Adding a co-worker

Open the presentation **Orgchart** saved in the last task.

1   Double click on the organisation chart to run Microsoft Organization Chart.

2   Click on the   **Co-worker to the right**   button and then click on the rightmost
     box of the second level to create an extra box at that level.

3   Add the following text to this box

     Sandra Jones
     Assistant Director
     Heritage and
     Libraries

4   Close the Microsoft Organization Chart, return to the slide and save the presenta-
     tion.

Task 5: Adding co-managers to a chart

Add a new organisation slide to the presentation **Orgchart**. The aim is to create the
structure shown below which has a co-manager level.

1   Add a new organisation slide to the presentation **Orgchart**.

2   Delete two of the lower level boxes by selecting them and pressing the *Delete*
     key. Note two boxes may be selected at once by holding down the *Shift* key
     during the selection process.

3   Click on the one remaining subordinate box and choose Co-manager from the
     Styles menu.

4   Click on the **Subordinate** button and then click on the top level box in the
     chart, thereby creating two co-managers.

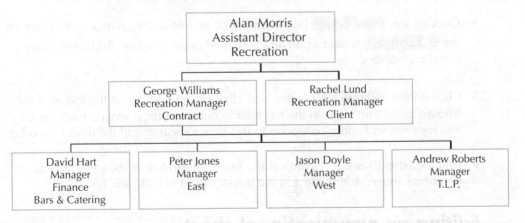

5   Change back to a normal hierarchical style by selecting the first button in the
     Styles menu. Click on Subordinate and add a subordinate to the co-managers by
     clicking on one of them. Repeat to add another three subordinates of the co-
     managers.

6   Add the text for names and positions as illustrated.

7   Close the Microsoft Organization Chart and save the presentation.

Task 6: Adding groups of co-workers

In this task the final slide in the presentation **Orgchart** will be created as illustrated.

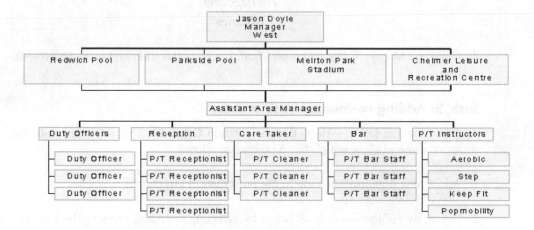

1   Add a new organisation slide to the presentation **Orgchart**.

2   To select the boxes at level 2 choose Edit-Select levels and choose 2 through 2.

3   Next open the Styles menu and select Co-managers. Choose a left co-worker and click on the leftmost co-manager to create four co-managers.

4   Click on the Subordinate button and click on one of the co-managers. Click on the Subordinate button again and add another subordinate. Add three additional co-workers.

5   Click on the Subordinate button and click on leftmost box at the lowest level. Choose Styles and click on the top middle button (vertical group). Click on Co-worker right and add a co-worker to this box. Repeat to add the third co-worker.

6   Add the other lowest level vertical groups, as illustrated, in the same way as described above. Add the text to the boxes, return to slide and save.

Editing an organisational chart

Text in the boxes in an organisational chart can be edited and its font, alignment, and colour can be altered using the Text menu. The colour, line style and shadow effects of the boxes can be changed using the Boxes menu. The background colour of the whole chart can be set using the Chart menu.

Task 7: Editing colours, line styles and shadows

1 In the Microsoft Organization Chart display the first slide of the presentation **Orgchart**. Select the top level box. Using Text-Font alter the font of the text. As the whole box is selected all the text in the box will reflect the change you make. Try selecting a portion of the text within the box and altering its font, you will find that only the selected text is changed.

2 Investigate changing the colour of the text using Text-Color.

3 Select all the boxes using Edit-Select Levels and change the colour of the box background using Boxes-Box Color. If you wish to experiment, then select different levels and apply different colours to the boxes; however, bear in mind that for a serious presentation too many colours will look gaudy so they should be chosen with care. If in doubt then choose fewer rather than more colours.

4 Select boxes and levels and investigate the options in the Boxes menu. Take care when choosing these for a serious presentation, err on the fewer effects side to avoid making your chart look too busy.

5 Finally through Chart-Background Color you may choose the background for the whole chart. When choosing this and other colours in the slide bear in mind the colours you have in your presentation template.

6 Experiment with this chart, return to the slide, save and experiment with changing text, colour and line style in the other two charts in this presentation.

7 To complete the presentation, choose a suitable title for it and, in Slide View, add this to a title slide at the beginning. Save the presentation as **Orgchart**.

Specialist slides and effects

What you will learn in this unit

This unit looks at some of the more specialist aspects of slide presentation creation. As the usage of these in presentations will more occasional, they are grouped together here. By the end of this unit you will be able to

- hide slides in a presentation
- create custom shows and agenda slides
- branch to other presentations or documents
- add equations to slides using the Equation Editor

and finally, to allow you to personalise the way you work with PowerPoint, you will start to

- customise toolbars.

Hiding slides

You may wish to show a similar but slightly different presentation to different audiences. There may be small differences such as one or two extra slides you wish to show to one audience but not to the other. To save having to create two presentations one for each audience PowerPoint allows you to choose whether or not to hide a slide during a presentation.

You may hide a slide as follows.

1   Display your presentation in Slide Sorter View and select the slide or slides that you wish to hide.

2   Click on the **Hide Slide** button. At the bottom right corner of the selected slides a **Hide** symbol appears . Click on a blank area of the screen to deselect the selected slide(s).

3   Click on the **Slide Show** button. Notice that the hidden slides do not appear in the presentation.

4   If you wish the slide to be hidden no longer, select it in Slide Sorter View and click on the **Hide Slide** button.

Displaying a hidden slide during a slide show

- Start the slide show. Start the slide show.Right-click the slide that precedes the hidden one, choose Go, and then select Hidden Slide; the command will be available only if the next slide is hidden.

■ *Alternatively*, right-click any slide in a presentation, choose Go, select Slide Navigator, and then double-click the slide you want. Numbers in parentheses designate hidden slides.

Task 1: Hiding a slide

1 Open the presentation **Project** in Slide Sorter View. Select slide the slide showing the layout plan.

2 Click on the ▌ **Hide Slide** ▌ button and run the presentation.

3 Re-run the presentation but this time right-click on the slide that appears before the layout plan. The hidden slide will then appear in the normal way.

4 Return to Slide Sorter View and 'unhide' the hidden slide.

Custom Slide Shows

PowerPoint comes with a new feature, called Custom Slide Shows, that allows you to create a presentation within a presentation. Instead of creating multiple, nearly identical presentations for different audiences, you can group together and name the slides that differ and then jump to these slides during your presentation.

For example, you might want to give a presentation to groups of people within the same organisation that are employed at different sites. The slide show includes, say, Slides 1 through 10, which are identical for all groups of employees, and several custom shows, each specific to a group of employees. You can show the first ten slides to any group and then jump to the particular custom show relevant to the target group.

You can jump to a custom show by using the Slide Show-Action Settings command to set up a hyperlink to the show. Or, during a presentation, you can right-click, point to Go on the shortcut menu, point to Custom Show, and then choose the name of the show you want to jump to.

After you create a custom show, you can edit it by adding or removing slides from the show.

You may create and edit a custom show as follows.

1 Create a presentation with all the slides that you will need. To group slides into custom shows choose Slide Show-Custom Shows, and choose New.

2 Under Slides in presentation, select the slides you want to include in the custom show, and then click on the ▌ **Add>>** ▌ button. To select multiple slides, hold down *Ctrl* as you click on each slide. The selected slides will appear in Slides in Custom Show.

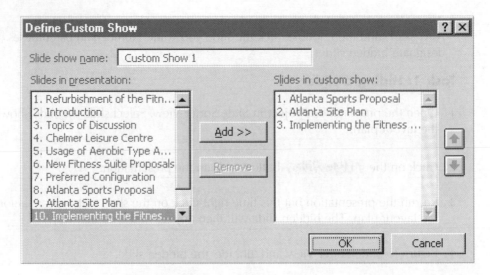

3   To change the order in which slides appear, select a slide, and then click one of the arrows to move the slide up or down in the list.

4   Type a name in the Slide show name box, and then click **OK** .

To see a preview of a custom show, select the name of the show in the Custom Shows dialog box, and then click on the **Show** button.

Agenda or summary slide

You can create a slide that lists agenda items or the main sections of your presentation, or that you can use as your home page on the Internet. With an agenda slide, you can jump to a related section in your presentation and then automatically return to the agenda slide when you reach the end of the section.

1   In Slide Sorter View, open the completed presentation you want to add an agenda slide to. Create a custom show for each topic you want on the agenda slide.

2   In slide sorter or outline view, hold down the *Shift* key and select the first slide in each custom show.

3   On the Slide Sorter or Outlining toolbar, click on the **Summary Slide** button.

4   A new slide, with bulleted titles from the selected slides, appears in front of the first selected slide.

5   Select the new slide, and then switch to Slide View.

6   To create a hyperlink from a bulleted item to a custom show, select the bulleted item, choose Slide Show-Action Settings.

7   With the **Mouse Click** tab selected choose the Hyperlink to option and select Custom Shows, in the Link to Custom Show dialog box that appears and then choose the name of the show you want to jump to. To return to the agenda slide after the last slide of the custom show, tick the Show and return check box at the bottom of the Link to Custom Show dialog box.

8   Repeat the last two steps for each bulleted item on the agenda slide. Save the presentation.

Task 2: Creating custom shows and an agenda (summary) slide

In this task the presentation **Project** will be divided into a set of small custom shows.

1   Open the presentation **Project** and save it as **Project (Custom Shows)**. View it in Slide Sorter View. Choose Slide Show-Custom Shows, and click on New.

2   Add Slides 2 to 4 to the slides in custom show by selecting them and clicking on the **Add>>** button. Keep the name **Custom Show 1** in the Slide show name box, and then click **OK**.

3   Repeat, adding Slides 5, 6 and 7 to **Custom Show 2**; 8, 9 and 10 to **Custom Show 3**; and lastly Slides 11 and 12 to **Custom Show 4**.

4   In Slide Sorter or Outline View, hold down the *Shift* key and select the first slide in each custom show, i.e. Slides 2, 5, 8 and 11. Click on the **Summary Slide** button: a new slide is added before the old Slide 2. Select this slide, and switch to Slide View.

Summary Slide

- Introduction
- Usage of Aerobic Type Activities
- Atlanta Sports Proposal
- Summary of Key Points

5   Select the first bulleted item, 'Introduction', and choose Slide Show-Action Settings.

6 With the **Mouse Click** tab selected choose the Hyperlink to option and select **Custom Show**, and then choose **Custom Show 1**. Tick the Show and return check box.

7 Repeat the last two steps for each bulleted item on the agenda slide. Save the presentation.

8 Run the presentation and test out the links.

Branching to another presentation or application

You may wish material that is held in another application or presentation to be available to your presentation. You might want to provide more detail on a topic by being able to branch to an Excel worksheet, for instance. This ability to look in more detail at a topic is known as 'drilling down'. You can set up either selected text or an object to act as the link to the other presentation or application.

Create a slide with a link to another PowerPoint presentation as follows.

1 Display the presentation in Slide View. Select the slide from which the link is to occur. Either add a text box with suitable text or add an object such as an Action button or AutoShape to the slide that is going to act as the link. Save the presentation, select the **Text Box** or **Autoshape** button and choose Slide show-Action Settings. With the **Mouse Click** tab selected choose the Hyperlink to option and select Other PowerPoint presentation from the list.

2 Select the presentation file you are currently working in and click on **OK**. Choose to link to a particular slide, usually slide 1, and click on **OK**. Click on **OK** in the Action Settings dialog box and save the presentation.

3 Show the presentation. On the link slide, click on the object you have used for your link. The presentation will branch to display the linked presentation.

4 Click to advance through the linked presentation at the end of which you will be returned to the original linking slide. You can then continue with that series of slides.

5 To delete a linking object simply select it and press *Delete*.

You may create a slide with a link to another application as follows.

1 Follow step 1 above except that the option choice is Other file rather than Other PowerPoint presentation.

2 Select the file you want to link to and click on **OK**. Click **OK** in the Action Settings dialog box and save the presentation.

If the document is, say, an Excel spreadsheet then you may work with this spreadsheet as you would do normally, allowing your audience to see your methods of analysis. When the demonstration has finished close the application and you are returned to your linking slide and can continue with the presentation.

Task 3: Branching to another presentation

For this task we will use two presentations **Project** and **Orgchart**.

1 Display the presentation **Project** in Slide View. Select the first slide and use the Draw toolbar to add a text box with the text **Organisational Structure**. Select this text box and choose Slide Show-Action Settings. With the **Mouse Click** tab selected choose the Hyperlink to option and select Other PowerPoint presentation from the list.

2 Select the file **Orgchart** (you may have to select the correct folder using the Look in box first) and click on **OK**. In the Hyperlink to Slide dialog box, select the first slide in that presentation and click on **OK**. Click **OK** in the Action Settings dialog box and save the presentation.

3 Show the presentation. On the link slide click on the linking text box (note that the text is underlined to indicate a link). The presentation will branch to display the presentation **Orgchart**. Click to advance through this presentation, at the end of which you will be returned to the original slide.

Adding equations

Equations may be added to a slide in the same way as any other object. Either double-clicking on an Object placeholder or using Insert-Object will generate the Object dialog box from which you select Microsoft Equation Editor 3.0. An Equation Editor window as illustrated below should open.

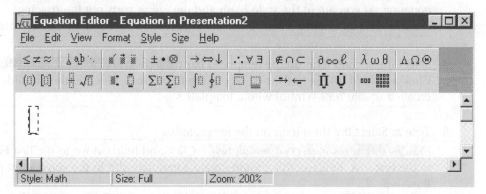

The Equation Editor window features its own menu and two palette bars. The two palette bars are the symbol palettes and the template palettes. Below is the workspace in which you build up your equation.

Building an equation

It is best to write down the equation to be created so that its method of construction can be considered. The basic rule for creating an equation is to set up a template first and then to fill the slots in the template with symbols. If the wrong template is inserted by mistake use Edit-Undo to remove it.

Templates are chosen from the lower palette bar. The icons in this bar represent the categories of template. By clicking and holding the mouse button on one of these icons a sub-menu appears showing all the templates available in that category. Still holding the mouse button down move to the one required and release the button. Symbols can be inserted into the template to complete the equation.

It is beyond the scope of this unit to go into very much detail concerning equation creation. However, by illustrating the creation of one basic equation, the equation editor will be introduced. Further tasks concerning the Equation Editor may be found in Word 97 Basic Skills.

Task 4: Adding an equation

The equation to be produced is that for calculating the hypotenuse of a right-angled triangle (Pythagoras' theorem).

$$c = \sqrt{a^2 + b^2}$$

1   Start a new presentation as a blank presentation and choose Object Layout from the New Slide Autolayout dialog box.

2   Double-click on the Object placeholder and select Microsoft Equation Editor 3.0. Note that you can move the Equation Editor window by dragging its title bar.

3   Type *c=*. It is worth noting at this point that you cannot type a space into an equation, as you are in the style Math and the Editor sorts out the spacing. However, if you choose a text rather than math style then spaces can be entered.

4   Select the second icon on the templates bar (**Fraction and Radical templates**). Click and hold. Move to the first box in the fourth row. Release; this should create a square root symbol with a template slot.

5   Type *a.* Select the third icon on the template bar (**Subscript and superscript templates**). Click and hold. Move to the first box in the first row. Release; this should create a template slot in the superscript position. Type *2*.

6   Move the insertion point to the right by pressing the right arrow key once. Type *+b* then add another superscript template and type *2*.

7   To embed the equation into the slide, choose File-Exit and Return to Presentation. You can move and size the equation object to suit.

8   If changes to the equation are required, double-click on it to invoke the Equation Editor. To make adjustments to the font and size of an equation use either Style-Define or Size-Define. The dialog boxes that these produce will allow different type fonts and sizes to be applied to the individual parts that make up an equation.

Customising toolbars

If you find you use a command often, you might want to set up the toolbars so they have precisely the buttons you want to use. This involves adding a button or buttons to an existing toolbar. If you want more customisation then you can build your own personalised toolbar, including your own choice of buttons.

You may add a button to a toolbar as follows.

1   Choose View-Toolbars-Customize. The Customize dialog box appears. Click on the **Commands** tab.

2   In the Categories box, select a tool category that includes the button you want to add. The buttons in the category appear on the right. A scroll bar appears on the right when there are more buttons in the selected category than the window will hold.

3   When you find the button you want to add, drag it and drop it on the toolbar where you want it. You can drag and drop as many buttons as you want.

4   When you finish adding buttons to toolbars, click on the **Close** button. You can now drag the edge of the toolbar to move it or change its shape if you want.

You may create a custom toolbar as follows.

1   Choose View-Toolbars-Customize. The Customize dialog box appears, select the **Toolbars** tab and click on the **New** button.

2   Key in a name for your new toolbar and click on **OK**. The new toolbar appears.

3   In the Customize dialog box, choose the **Commands** tab. In the Categories box, select a tool category that includes the button you want to add. The buttons in the category appear on the right.

4   When you find the button you want to add, drag it to the new toolbar and drop the button onto the toolbar. The button is added to the toolbar.

5   Drag as many buttons as you want to your Custom toolbar. You can now move the toolbar and change its shape if you want.

Creating custom slide designs

What you will learn in this unit

In the preceding units you have seen how to apply a slide design to a presentation. There are only a limited number of slide designs supplied with PowerPoint, so you may wish to customise these or even start with a blank slide and design your own design template. Some of the design templates that are available with PowerPoint have animation; it is possible to customise this or to create your own animation effects.

Alternatively, you may have an earlier version of PowerPoint and want to use a design template from that version. It is possible save and adapt these as PowerPoint 97 design templates. By the end of this unit you will be able to:

- create a slide design from an existing design
- create a slide design from a blank presentation
- add animation to a slide design
- convert a slide template from an older version of PowerPoint to a new design template.

Creating design templates

Slide designs or templates are saved as separate files, usually in one of the template folders. They have the extension .pot and contain the design information for any presentation that is to be based on them. This includes any background graphics, animations, sound effects, colour schemes, text fonts, bullet styles and positions of placeholders. The design information is held in the Masters: Slide, Title, Notes and Handout Masters. You can create designs for all or some of these Masters and save them as a design template.

A design template can be created from an existing template or can be completely new. You may create a design template from an existing one as follows.

1   Open an existing presentation that is based on the design you wish to modify. Alternatively, starting with a blank presentation, apply a design template to create a presentation as a basis for your new design template.

2   Change the template to suit your needs. For example, change the colour scheme, or use the slide master to change items on the background or the appearance of the font.

3   Choose File-Save As, enter a name for your design template, and then select Presentation templates in the Save as type box.

You can save your new design template in one of your own folders, or you can save it with the other design templates in the Presentation Designs folder.

If none of the templates suits your needs, or you want to create a presentation with a unique appearance, start with a blank presentation. To open the blank presentation, choose File-New, and then click the **General** tab. Follow the steps above to create your own design.

Task 1: Creating a design from an existing design

In this task we shall investigate altering the colours used in an existing slide design and will save the design with the new colours as a new design template.

1 Open a blank presentation and add a title slide. Choose Apply Design from the shortcut menu (accessed by clicking on the right hand mouse button) and select the design Zesty.

2 Display the Title Master via View Master-Title Master and click on the background so that it is selected (handles appear at edge of slide). Choose Draw-Ungroup and you will see more handles. Click outside the slide to deselect these and then click on the striped section and use Draw-Ungroup to ungroup these.

3 Apply colours of your choice to the rectangles and group the set of stripes and then group all the rectangles.

4 Apply a font of your choice to the titles.

5 Display the Slide Master (View Master-Title Master) and alter the colours in this as for the Title Master. Apply a font of your choice to the titles.

6 If you wish, choose Format-Slide Color Scheme and make any alterations in keeping with the colours you have chosen for the background.

7 Using File-Save As save the design by selecting Presentation templates from the Save as type box, choosing a suitable folder (make a note of where you have stored the design), and with the name **Myzesty.pot**. Close the presentation.

8 To use this design, start a new presentation, and select Apply Design from the General tab in the New Presentations dialog box. Choose **Myzesty**. Create the following slides and examine the application of the design.

Task 2: Creating a design starting with a blank presentation

In this task a slide design that might be used by an Estate Agent or other organisation in the building trade is to be created. It introduces the concept of how a striking design can be created from some fairly simple graphics.

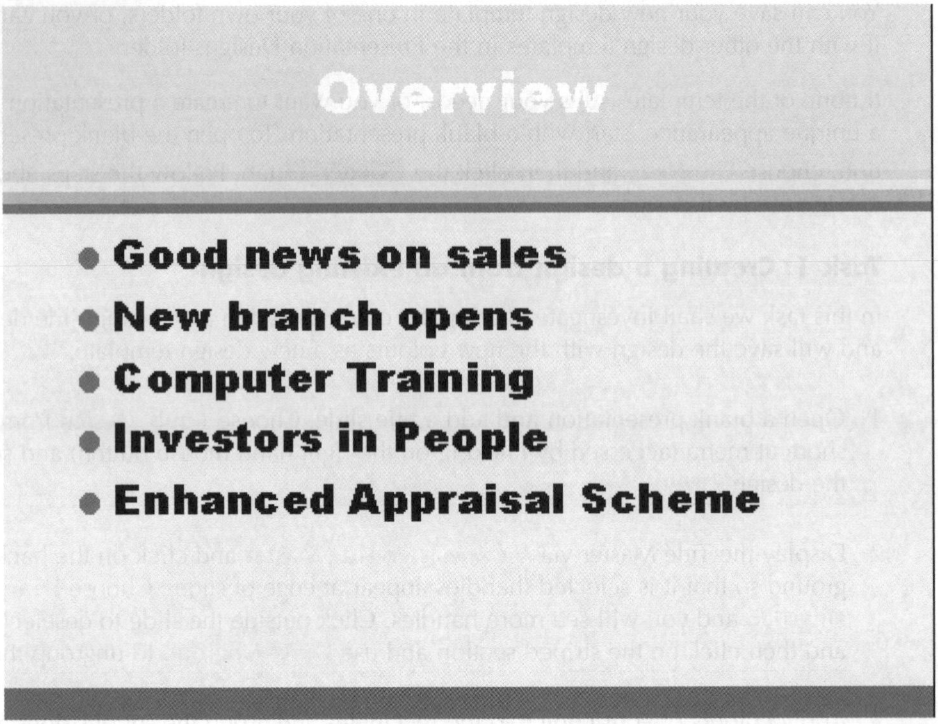

Overview

- **Good news on sales**
- **New branch opens**
- **Computer Training**
- **Investors in People**
- **Enhanced Appraisal Scheme**

1   Open a blank presentation and add a title slide. Display the Slide Master. Add a Title Master using Insert-New Title Master.

2   Using the illustration on the following page as a guide, add some diagonally shaded fill (brown) to the Title Master and add some rectangles in one corner to produce a brick wall effect. The half-bricks were created using a FreeForm shape (see Unit 13). Fill the bricks with a brown colour. If you use custom colours you can vary the shades of brown, to give a more natural effect or you could investigate a textured or patterned fill.

3   Make any suitable changes to the text font and the positions of the placeholders.Click on **Apply** .

4   Select all the bricks (click on them one by one with the *Shift* key held down) and copy them using Edit-Copy. Display the Slide Master and paste in the bricks using Edit-Paste. While they are all selected move them to, say, the bottom right hand corner of the Slide Master.

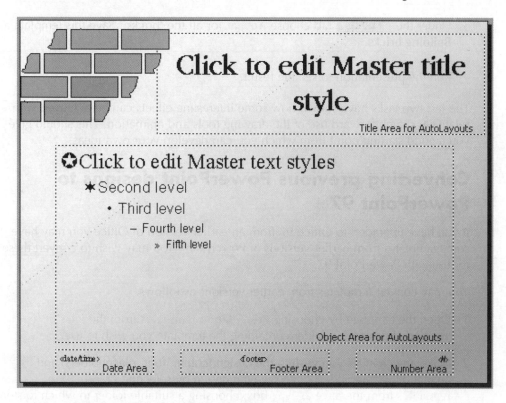

5   Add a shaded fill to the Slide Master and make any changes you think suitable to the text font and the positions of the placeholders. Click on **Apply**.

6   Save this as a presentation design template, **Bricks.pot**, close it and try it out by creating the first two slides from the **Briefing** presentation.

Task 3: Adding animation to a design

The aim of this task is to add animation to the design template created in the last task. The animation will only be added to the Title Master, and aims to give the effect of the wall being built brick by brick. An interesting or unusual effect at the beginning of a presentation could help to engage the audience's attention, but effects repeated through a presentation rapidly become boring, so remember to keep your target audience in mind when choosing effects in a presentation.

1   Open the template **Bricks** by choosing Presentation Templates from the Files of type box. If the Title Master is not displayed then display it.

2   Choose Slide Show-Custom animation. Under the **Timing** tab select all the drawing objects in the 'brick wall' and set animation timing to automatically after one second. Using the arrows next to the Animation Order box, adjust the animation order so that you start with the bottom layer of bricks and build upwards.

3 Under the █Effects█ tab choose Appear for all the 'bricks'. Save this template as **Building bricks**.

4 Run the presentation to see the result.

The last two tasks have shown how some interesting effects can be achieved with relatively straightforward use of the drawing tools and animation. This should give you a good starting point from which you can develop your own ideas.

Converting previous PowerPoint designs to PowerPoint 97

If you have upgraded to Office 97 from an earlier version of Office you may have some templates from earlier versions of PowerPoint. You may wish to convert these for use with PowerPoint 97.

You may convert templates from earlier versions as follows.

1 Open the template by choosing Presentation templates from the Files of type box and choosing the folder containing the template you wish to use.

2 Make any changes you wish to the design, colour, font, placeholders, and animation. Using File-Save As save the design by selecting Presentation templates from the Save as type box, choosing a suitable folder in which to store the design. If you wish, you can overwrite the old design with the new one but check that you no longer want the old design first.

PowerPoint Viewer and Internet links

What you will learn in this unit

This unit may be omitted if you do not need to display presentations on a remote computer which does not have PowerPoint installed, or if you do not have Internet connection.

PowerPoint provides a program known as the PowerPoint Viewer that allows you to run presentations on computers that do not have PowerPoint installed. However, the remote computer needs Windows 95 or NT. This would be particularly useful if you were advertising a product or service and wished to distribute on-screen presentations on floppy disk or over a network.

As with all Office 97 applications, PowerPoint provides an easy way to browse other documents (locally or on the World Wide Web) through the Web toolbar. We have already seen, in Unit 18, how to link to other documents and now this can be extended to link to documents on the Internet.

By the end of this unit you will be able to:

- use the PowerPoint Viewer
- use the Web toolbar
- add Internet links to a presentation.

Using the PowerPoint Viewer

The PowerPoint Viewer can be added to the same disk as a presentation by using the Pack and Go Wizard. Then you can unpack the Viewer and presentation together and run the slide show on another computer. You can also create a play list to use with the Viewer so you can run multiple presentations, one after another.

The Viewer, which can be freely distributed with no additional licence, comes with PowerPoint and is located in the Office 97 ValuPack folder on the CD-ROM. If you did not install PowerPoint from a CD-ROM but you have access to the World Wide Web you can download the Viewer from the Microsoft Web site.

The Viewer that comes with PowerPoint 97 supports all PowerPoint 95 features and can be used with both PowerPoint for Windows and the Macintosh.

Packing up a presentation

You may pack up a presentation for use on another computer as follows.

1   Open the presentation you want to save to a disk. Choose File-Pack and Go. The Pack and Go Wizard starts. Click on   Next> .

2 The Active presentation option should be selected, click on **Next>** . Note that you can choose an alternative presentation at this point by browsing for it.

3 Select the drive to which the file should be copied. This is usually the a: drive, if you are sending or taking disks to the remote computer. You can save the files on your local hard drive if you intend to attach it to an e-mail message to a recipient without PowerPoint.

4 Choose whether or not to include linked files and to embed TrueType fonts. Include TrueType fonts if you think the remote computer will not have the range of fonts that your computer has. You should include linked files if you have used them in your presentation, if you do not the links will not work at the remote computer.

5 If the remote computer does not have PowerPoint installed then you must choose the View for Windows 95 or NT option. Including the Viewer gives full support for the features in PowerPoint 97. Click on **Finish** to save the file. If you have chosen the option to include the Viewer then you may need to insert the Office CD-ROM so that the Viewer program can be included.

6 If your presentation is large and you are saving to floppy disk then you will be prompted to insert extra floppy disks. Your presentation is saved as a compressed file and there is also a setup file saved, **Pngsetup**, that you will need to run to unpack (and display, if the Viewer is included) your presentation on the remote computer.

Unpacking a presentation at a remote computer

You may unpack a presentation to run on another computer.

Before you can do this procedure, you must have used the Pack and Go Wizard to package your presentation; as explained above.

1 Insert the disk onto which you have copied your presentation.

2 In Windows Explorer, select the drive where the disk is located, and then double-click **Pngsetup**. This will start the program that unpacks the presentation and the Viewer.

3 Enter the destination you want to copy the presentation to; this will be a directory (folder) on the remote computer's hard disk, which ideally should be empty.

4 To run the slide show, in Explorer, double-click the PowerPoint Viewer program file, **Ppview32**, to start the Viewer. Select the presentation you want to run.

Although a task is not given here you may experiment with using Pack and Go using one of the presentations we have created, such as **Advert**.

PowerPoint and the Internet

PowerPoint can be used to open presentations on an Intranet (a local Web), or if you are connected, on the Internet (World Wide Web). PowerPoint will allow you to open Web documents that are in an HTML format.

The Web toolbar, which you will find in all Office 97 applications, makes it easy to access documents on an Intranet or on the Internet. The Web toolbar allows you to open, search and browse through any presentation or Web page. To display the Web toolbar click on the Web toolbar button on the **Standard** toolbar.

To open a document, type in its address to the Address text box at the end of the toolbar. If you are looking for a local presentation you might type *My documents\presentations\advert.ppt*. If you are looking for a document on the Internet, type in the address (URL) of that document. Addresses that you enter can be retained so that you can open the address list and select the document you want.

If the document you are opening is in HTML format, your browser will start to display it. If the document is a Word document then Word will start so that the document is displayed.

Task 1: Using the Web toolbar

1 Click on the **Web** toolbar button to display the Web toolbar.

2 Using Go-Open click on the **Browse** button and open a presentation. Notice that you can only view the presentation.

3 If you try opening other kinds of documents e.g. a Word document, they will be opened in their associated application.

Hyperlinks to the Internet

Adding a hyperlink to your presentation that you can use to jump to an address on the Internet is essentially the same as adding a link that jumps to a custom show, a specific slide within your presentation, a different presentation altogether, a Word document or a Microsoft Excel spreadsheet. These links were discussed in Unit 18.

You can create a hyperlink from any text or object and then you can click on the hyperlink to start its action. Text that represents a hyperlink appears underlined and in a colour that co-ordinates with the presentation colour scheme. The colour changes after you jump from a hyperlink, so you can tell which hyperlinks you have already viewed.

When you are adding hyperlinks to locations on the Internet, you can use the Web toolbar to browse for links and add interesting files to the Favorites folder. You will find a history of the presentations and you are jumping to and from in the drop down list at the end of the toolbar. The Web toolbar keeps a list of the last ten addresses you used the toolbar or a hyperlink to jump to, making it easy to return to any presentation or document on the list.

You may add a hyperlink to the Internet as follows.

1   Open the presentation and add the link text or object.

2   Select the link text or object and using Slide Show-Action Settings, select Hyperlink to and choose URL and enter the address of the presentation or document you wish to link to.

Presentations on the Internet

If you have access to the Internet you can open presentations on the World Wide Web or anywhere on the Internet using File-Open in any of your Office programs. If your organisation has an Intranet, you can open presentations there as well. In addition, if you have access rights to save files on your Internet or Intranet server, you can save presentations using File-Save As.

The Web toolbar is available in all Office applications, not just PowerPoint, making it easy to browse through presentations and other Office documents that contain hyperlinks.

Saving a presentation in HTML format

If you want to publish a presentation on the Web in HTML format, PowerPoint allows you to save any existing presentation in HTML format for viewing on the Web.

You may save an existing presentation in HTML format as follows.

1   Open an existing presentation and choose File-Save as HTML. The Save as HTML Wizard starts. Click on Next> .

2   Choose New Layout and click on Next> . Other layouts are available once you have used the Wizard and saved the settings that you specify (see Step 9).

3   Choose either Standard or Browser Frames for the page style. If you are not sure then choose Standard. Click on Next> .

4   Choose the type of graphics format. You can choose from gif, jpg or PowerPoint animation. On the Web, graphics are commonly saved in gif format but jpg is equally suitable. If your presentation contains animations then try choosing PowerPoint animation. Click on Next> .

5   Accept the resolution options unless you know that you wish to choose a higher resolution. It is better to make your Web pages viewable by as many browsers as possible.

6   You may add your e-mail address and the address of your home page (if you have one). If you wish the viewer to be able to download the original presentation then click in the Download original presentation check box.

7   Accept the standard browser colours, unless you want to customise colours for links and visited links, and click on `Next>`.

8   Select a button style and click on `Next>`. Choose the positioning of the navigation buttons and whether to include the slide notes in the Web pages. Click on `Next>`.

9   Choose a folder (directory) in which to save the pages. The pages and associated graphics files and the presentation file will be saved in a sub-folder created from this folder. Click on `Next>`. The Wizard now has all the information it needs so click on `Finish` to save the presentation in HTML format. PowerPoint gives you the opportunity to save the HTML conversion settings so that you can use them again.

10 View the presentation using your browser starting with the index.htm page. The Animation Viewer can be downloaded from the Internet by clicking on the appropriate graphic on the index page. All the files in the new directory should be uploaded to your Web server for the presentation to be available on the Internet or Intranet.

No task is given here but you could try saving the presentation **Briefing** in HTML format. View the result with your browser.

Basic Windows Operations

Some readers will not be familiar with Windows '95 and so PowerPoint may be one of the first Windows 95 applications encountered by these users. Any reader who has not previously used Windows 95 is strongly recommended to run through the Windows tutorial which introduces users to mouse techniques and the basic operation of Windows. This tutorial can be found by clicking on the Start button on the taskbar, selecting Help, clicking on the Contents tab and selecting Tour: Ten minutes to using Windows. This appendix briefly summarises some of the key operations and should act as a ready reference to some of the terminology that is used elsewhere in the book.

Mouse Techniques

The basic mouse techniques are listed in the table below, with a simple description of each technique.

To	Do This
Point	Position the mouse pointer on or next to something.
Click	Position the pointer and then quickly press and release the left mouse button.
Double click	Position the pointer and then quickly press and release the left mouse button twice.
Triple click	Position the pointer and then quickly press and release the left mouse button three times.
Drag	Position the pointer. Press and hold down the left mouse button as you move the mouse to the desired position. The release the button.

Mouse Pointer Shapes

When the mouse is pointed to different parts of the screen, the pointer shape changes allowing you to perform different tasks. Some commands also change the pointer shape.

The table on the following page lists some common pointer shapes as encountered in Powerpoint.

Pointer shape	*Meaning*
I	The pointer over the text area. Click to position an insertion point where text may be typed.
⬚	The pointer appears over menus, non-text areas of windows, inactive windows, scroll bars, or toolbar. You can choose a menu and command or click a button. You can use the pointer to drag to make a selection.
✛	In Outline View, this appears in the left selection area and allows selection and moving of parts of a presentation. When clicked on, the ▐ Slide ▐ icon will select that slide.
✛	In Outline view, this appears when a selection is being dragged. A horizontal line indicates the drop position.
⧗	PowerPoint is performing a task that will take a few seconds.
╪ ╫	Appears along the borders between columns and rows when editing an embedded Word table. Drag to resize the column or row.
⬇	This pointer appears at the top of a column while editing an embedded Word table. Click to select the column.
⬚?	The pointer appears after you press *Shift-F1*. You can point to any item on the screen and click to view specific Help.
⬚	This 'drag and drop' pointer appears when you make a selection and drag the selection to its new location, releasing the mouse button to drop or insert the selection.
↕ ↔ ⤢ ⤡	The pointer is on an object sizing handle. Depending on which handle is chosen the pointer will assume one of the shapes opposite. Drag to resize the object.
⊥	This pointer appears when the text tool has been chosen. Click to position the control or drag to draw a text box.

Pointer shape	Meaning
+	This pointer appears when a drawing tool has been selected. Drag the shape selected.
	This shape appears when the Free Rotate tool is chosen when a drawing tool is selected.
	The pointer is on a window border. Depending on which border the pointer will assume one of the shapes opposite. Drag to resize the window.
	This pointer appears when you have selected the Move or Size command from the Control menu. You can move the window to a new position or drag the window border.

Basics of Windows 95

The following are the elements of a basic Windows 95 screen.

Menu Bar

The menu bar shows the titles of the various pull down menus that are available with a given application. To select a menu option, first select the menu by placing the mouse pointer over the name of the menu on the menu bar and click the left mouse button. The menu will appear. Move the mouse pointer to the menu option you require and click the left mouse button again. Note that any menu options displayed in light grey are not currently available. Menus can also be accessed via the keyboard. For example, to select the file menu press *Alt+F* i.e. press *Alt* together with the initial letter of the menu option.

Control Menu

The Control menu is found on all windows whether they are application windows or document windows. To access the Control menu click on the Control Menu box in the upper left corner of the window, or press *Alt+Spacebar*. The exact contents are different for different windows, but typically basic windows operations such as restore, move, size, minimise, maximise, close and switch to are represented.

Title Bar

The title bar tells you which window is displayed. By pointing the mouse at the window's title bar, and then dragging the title bar to a new location the window can removed.

Task Bar

At the bottom of your screen is the taskbar. It contains the [**Start**] button, which you can use to quickly start a program or to find a file. It's also the fastest way to get Help.

When you open a program, document, or window, a button appears on the taskbar. You can use this button to quickly switch between the windows you have open.

Maximize, Minimize and Restore Buttons

Clicking on the [**Maximize**] button enlarges a window to its maximum size, so that is fills the whole desktop.

Clicking on the [**Restore**] button will restore a maximised window to its previous size.

Clicking on the [**Minimize**] button reduces the window to a small icon at the bottom of the screen. When you shrink an application window to an icon, the application is still running in memory, but its window is not taking up space on your desktop.

Clicking on the [**Close**] button closes the window.

Dialog Boxes

Windows uses dialog boxes to request information from you and to provide information to you. Most dialog boxes include options, with each option asking for a different kind of information.

After all the requested information has been supplied, you choose a command button to carry out the command. Two command buttons that commonly feature on dialog boxes are **OK** and **Cancel** . **OK** causes the command to be executed. **Cancel** cancels the operation and removes the dialog box from the screen. These buttons represent the two means of quitting from a dialog box. To choose a command button, click on it, or if the button is currently active, press *Enter*.

There are a number of different kinds of dialog box.

Text boxes are boxes where you are allowed to type in text, such as a filename. The presence of a flashing vertical bar, or the insertion point, indicates that the text box is active and that you may enter text. If the text box is not active, place the mouse pointer on the box and click. The insertion point will then appear in the box.

List boxes show a column of available choices. Items can be selected from a list box by double clicking on the item, or clicking once on the item and then clicking on the **OK** button.

Check boxes offer a list of options that you can switch on and off. You can select as many or as few check box options as are applicable. When an option in a check box is selected it contains a ✓; otherwise the box is empty. To select a check box, click on the empty box.

151

Option buttons appear as a list of mutually exclusive items. You can select only one option from the list at a time. You can change a selection by selecting a different button. The selected button contains a black dot. To select an option button, click on it.

Scroll bars appear at the side of windows and list boxes. They appear when the information contained in a window cannot be displayed wholly within that window. Both vertical and horizontal scroll bars may be present depending on whether the document is too long or too wide to fit on the screen. The small box in the middle of the bar represents the position of the currently displayed text within the whole document. You can move to a different position in the text by moving this box. You can move this box either by clicking on the scroll bar arrow boxes, clicking on the scroll bar itself, or dragging the box.

PowerPoint toolbars

Standard toolbar

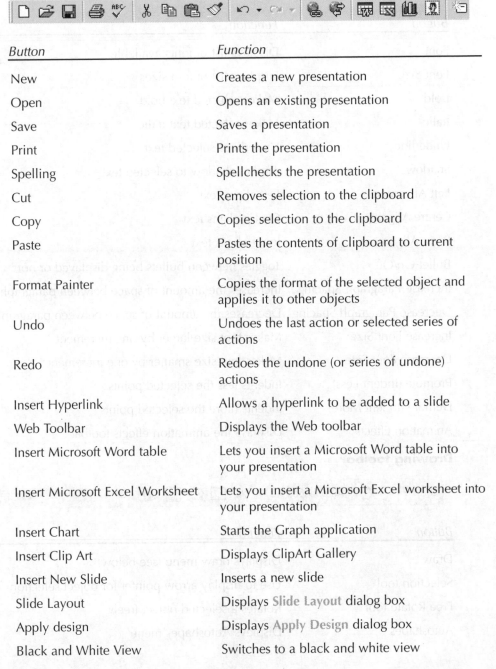

Button	Function
New	Creates a new presentation
Open	Opens an existing presentation
Save	Saves a presentation
Print	Prints the presentation
Spelling	Spellchecks the presentation
Cut	Removes selection to the clipboard
Copy	Copies selection to the clipboard
Paste	Pastes the contents of clipboard to current position
Format Painter	Copies the format of the selected object and applies it to other objects
Undo	Undoes the last action or selected series of actions
Redo	Redoes the undone (or series of undone) actions
Insert Hyperlink	Allows a hyperlink to be added to a slide
Web Toolbar	Displays the Web toolbar
Insert Microsoft Word table	Lets you insert a Microsoft Word table into your presentation
Insert Microsoft Excel Worksheet	Lets you insert a Microsoft Excel worksheet into your presentation
Insert Chart	Starts the Graph application
Insert Clip Art	Displays ClipArt Gallery
Insert New Slide	Inserts a new slide
Slide Layout	Displays Slide Layout dialog box
Apply design	Displays Apply Design dialog box
Black and White View	Switches to a black and white view

153

| Zoom | Use to set the magnification of the view |
| Office Assistant | Displays the Office Assistant through which help is available |

Formatting toolbar

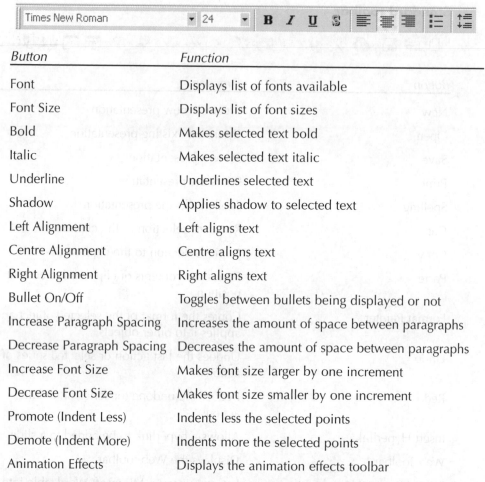

Button	Function
Font	Displays list of fonts available
Font Size	Displays list of font sizes
Bold	Makes selected text bold
Italic	Makes selected text italic
Underline	Underlines selected text
Shadow	Applies shadow to selected text
Left Alignment	Left aligns text
Centre Alignment	Centre aligns text
Right Alignment	Right aligns text
Bullet On/Off	Toggles between bullets being displayed or not
Increase Paragraph Spacing	Increases the amount of space between paragraphs
Decrease Paragraph Spacing	Decreases the amount of space between paragraphs
Increase Font Size	Makes font size larger by one increment
Decrease Font Size	Makes font size smaller by one increment
Promote (Indent Less)	Indents less the selected points
Demote (Indent More)	Indents more the selected points
Animation Effects	Displays the animation effects toolbar

Drawing toolbar

Button	Function
Draw	Displays draw menu (see below)
Selection tool	Use to display arrow pointer for object selection
Free Rotate tool	Rotates a selected object freely
Autoshapes	Displays Autoshapes menu

Button	Function
Line tool	Use to draw line
Arrow tool	Use to draw an arrow
Rectangle tool	Use to draw rectangle or square
Ellipse tool	Use to draw ellipse or circle
Text tool	Create text or text box on slide
Insert Word Art	Use to add WordArt
Fill Colour	Displays a drop-down choice of fill colours for the selected object
Line Colour	Displays a drop-down choice of colours for the selected line or edge
Font Colour	Displays a drop-down choice of colours for the selected font
Line Style	Displays a menu of line styles
Dash Style	Displays a menu of dash styles
Arrow Style	Displays a menu of arrow styles
Shadow	Displays a choice of various shadow effects
3-D	Displays a choice of various 3-D effects

Draw menu

Button	Function	
	Group, Ungroup, Regroup	Works with a selected set of objects by grouping or ungrouping them
Order		
	Bring to Front, Send to Back, Bring Forward, Send Backward	Controls layered position of selected item
	Bring in Front of Text, Send Behind Text	Brings the selected drawing object in front of or behind the text
	Grid	Allows options for grid to be set for aligning drawing objects

Nudge

⊞ ⊡ ⊞ ⊞   **Up, Down, Left, Right**   Nudges selected object up, down, left, or right

Align or distribute

🖿 🖿 🖿   **Align Left, Centre, Right**   Aligns selected objects to the left, centrally around a vertical axis, or to the right

🖿 🖿 🖿   **Align Top, Middle, Bottom**   Aligns selected objects to the top, centrally around a horizontal axis, or to the bottom

🖿 🖿   **Distribute Horizontally, Vertically**   Spaces selected object evenly

Rotate or flip

🖿   **Free Rotate**   Rotates the selected drawing object freely to any angle

🖿 🖿   **Rotate Left, Right**   Rotates the selected drawing object 90 degrees to the left or right

🖿 🖿   **Flip Horizontal, Vertical**   Flips the selected drawing object from left to right or top to bottom

Reroute connections   Updates the selected connections so that a connecting line takes the shortest route between the shapes it connects (without crossing either)

🖿   **Edit points**   Displays the vertices on Freeform objects so they may be reshaped

Autoshapes menu

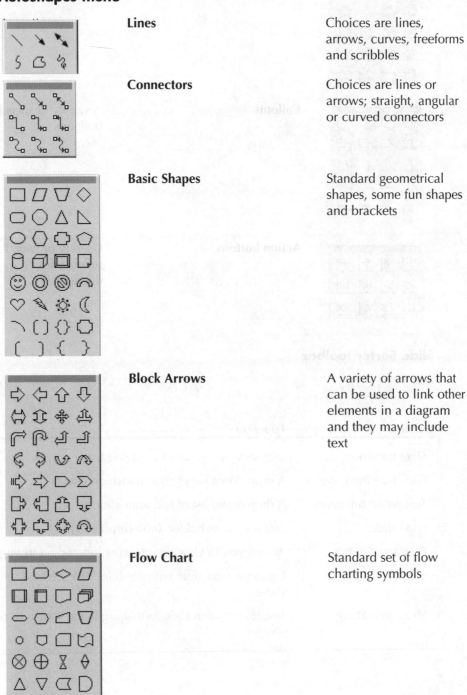

Lines

Choices are lines, arrows, curves, freeforms and scribbles

Connectors

Choices are lines or arrows; straight, angular or curved connectors

Basic Shapes

Standard geometrical shapes, some fun shapes and brackets

Block Arrows

A variety of arrows that can be used to link other elements in a diagram and they may include text

Flow Chart

Standard set of flow charting symbols

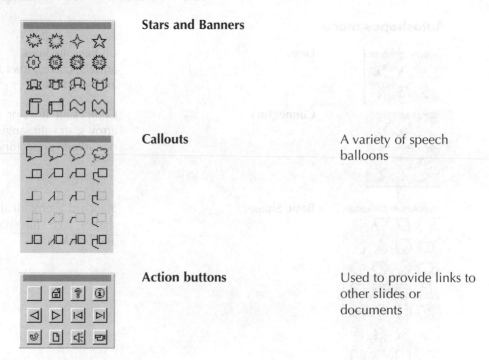

Stars and Banners

Callouts

A variety of speech balloons

Action buttons

Used to provide links to other slides or documents

Slide Sorter toolbar

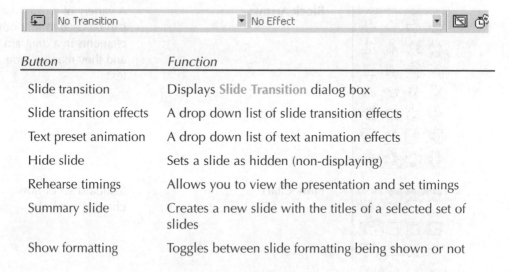

Button	Function
Slide transition	Displays Slide Transition dialog box
Slide transition effects	A drop down list of slide transition effects
Text preset animation	A drop down list of text animation effects
Hide slide	Sets a slide as hidden (non-displaying)
Rehearse timings	Allows you to view the presentation and set timings
Summary slide	Creates a new slide with the titles of a selected set of slides
Show formatting	Toggles between slide formatting being shown or not